Bloomsbury Heritage

ELIZABETH FRENCH BOYD

Bloomsbury Heritage

THEIR MOTHERS AND THEIR AUNTS

HAMISH HAMILTON

LONDON

First published in Great Britain 1976
by Hamish Hamilton Ltd
90 Great Russell Street London WC1B 3PT

Copyright © 1976 by Elizabeth French Boyd

SBN 241 89406 9

Printed in Great Britain by
Western Printing Services Ltd, Bristol

To the memory
of
Philippa Strachey
and
Marjorie Strachey

CONTENTS

ILLUSTRATIONS

Between pages 84 and 85

Gray (on the ground), Mrs. Strachey, Mrs. Gray, Dr. Lambourne, Gen. Strachey, and Dr. Hayden. By permission of
the Gray Herbarium, Harvard University.

11 The annual united march of Women's Suffrage groups in
London, 1908. Lady Strachey is in the front of the procession.
By permission of the Fawcett Library.

12 Anne Isabella Thackeray, Lady Ritchie. Portrait by Sargent (1914). By permission of Belinda Norman-Butler.

13 Mrs. Richmond Ritchie (*née* Anne Isabella Thackeray); a
photograph taken by Lord Battersea at Overstrand, about
1902. By permission of Belinda Norman-Butler.

14 Mary Warre-Cornish MacCarthy; portrait by Neville
Lytton. By permission of Lady David Cecil.

15 Mrs. Desmond MacCarthy (*née* Mary Warre-Cornish), a
snapshot of her playing croquet at Newington House, the
home of Ethel Sands, in 1913. From the collection of Lady
Ottoline Morrell, by permission of Julian Morrell Vinogradoff.

16 Molly MacCarthy, her daughter Rachel (Lady David
Cecil), and Ralph Partridge. A shapshot taken by Frances
Partridge. By permission of Frances Marshall Partridge.

17 The Memoir Club, in session about 1943. A painting by
Vanessa Bell. From left to right: Duncan Grant, Leonard
Woolf, Vanessa Bell, Clive Bell, David Garnett, J. M.
Keynes, Lydia Keynes, Desmond MacCarthy (reading a
memoir), Molly MacCarthy, Quentin Bell, and E. M.
Forster. The portraits, also from left to right, are of Virginia
Woolf, Lytton Strachey, and Roger Fry, the deceased mem-
bers. By permission of Mrs. David Garnett and kindness of
Professor Quentin Bell.

ACKNOWLEDGMENTS

I am obliged and deeply grateful to the many persons who have helped me in this study, with advice and testimony, sometimes with the loan of unpublished manuscripts, and with other encouragements and material aids. I wish to record my obligation to Professor and Mrs. Quentin Bell, Sir Geoffrey Keynes, the late Michael MacCarthy, Mrs. Frances Partridge, and the late Alix Strachey for the right to quote from unpublished manuscripts that are or have been in their possession. I am particularly indebted not only to them but also to the following persons for many favours and sometimes hours of their time and attention: Lord Annan, Miss Betty Askwith, Lord and Lady David Cecil, Miss Gwenda David, Professor Ruth Emery, Mrs. Dora Pattle Flynn, of Montreal, and her mother, the late Jane Gordon-Wright, Mr. Brian Hill, Mr. Michael Holroyd, Mr. John Lehmann, Dr. Dermod MacCarthy, the late Sir John Murray, Mrs. Belinda Norman-Butler, Miss Lucy Norton, Mr. Roger Temple Pattle, Miss Pamela Redmayne, Professor C. Richard Sanders, the late James Strachey and his sisters, the late Marjorie and Philippa Strachey, Mrs. Julian Morrell Vinogradoff, the late Joan Wake, and the late Leonard Woolf.

For permission to quote from copyrighted material, I am grateful to: Mrs. Belinda Norman-Butler (*The Letters and Private Papers of W. M. Thackeray*, ed. Gordon N. Ray, and the works of Anne Thackeray Ritchie and Hester Thackeray Fuller); Mr. Lovat Dickson (*Memories and Reflections*, by Lady Troubridge); Herr Helmut Gernsheim (his biography, *Julia Margaret Cameron*); Constable & Co., Ltd. (*Personal Reminiscences of Augusta Becher, 1830–1888*, ed. H. G. Rawlinson, © 1930); Gerald Duckworth & Co., Ltd. (*Life and Letters of Leslie Stephen*, by F. W. Maitland); Hart-Davis MacGibbon Ltd. (*Leslie Stephen: His Thought and Character in Relation to His Time*, by Noel Annan); The Hogarth Press (*Virginia Woolf, A Biography*, Vol. I, by Quentin Bell); The

Hogarth Press and the Literary Estate of Leonard Woolf (*Sowing* and *Beginning Again*); The Hogarth Press and the Literary Estate of Virginia Woolf (*Night and Day, The Moment and Other Essays, A Writer's Diary,* and *To the Lighthouse*); Harcourt Brace Jovanovich, Inc. (*To the Lighthouse* by Virginia Woolf, copyright, 1927, by Harcourt Brace Jovanovich, Inc., copyright, 1955, by Leonard Woolf. Reprinted by permission of the publishers); Longman Group Limited (*Men and Matters*, by Wilfrid Ward, and *Impressions That Remained*, by Dame Ethel Mary Smyth); Alfred A. Knopf, Inc. (*Impressions That Remained*, by Dame Ethel Mary Smyth, 2nd ed., 1946); Macmillan London and Basingstoke (*George Frederic Watts; Annals of an Artist's Life,* by M. S. Watts); G. P. Putnam's Sons (*Men and Memories; Recollections of William Rothenstein, 1872–1900,* by William Rothenstein, © 1931); and A. P. Watt & Son and the Estate of E. F. Benson (*As We Were,* by E. F. Benson).

Over the years I have received much help from the staffs of a number of libraries in this country and in England, and I wish to acknowledge my indebtedness to them; the staff members of Rutgers University and Douglass College libraries, of the Huntington, the Newberry, and the John Crear Libraries, the Houghton, Weidner, and Gray Herbarium Libraries of Harvard University, the library of Hamilton College, the New York Public Library, especially the Berg Collection, and in England, the British Museum, the London, and the Fawcett Libraries, and King's College Library, Cambridge University. I am also very grateful to the Research Council of Rutgers University for granting me leave of absence twice to pursue these studies.

Especially I want to thank a number of friends and former colleagues and teachers, who have read some or all of this book in its preparation and have given me the benefit of their expert advice and sometimes their research assistance. Professor Raymond M. Bennett, Miss Gladys M. Brownell, Miss Lillian B. Goodhart, Miss Winifred Halsted, Professor Serena Sue Hilsinger, Professor Muriel J. Hughes, Professor Julia H. Hysham, and Professor Susanne Howe Nobbe. Any errors or infelicities that have persisted I claim entirely for my own.

Highland Park, New Jersey
December 1975

I

Prologue: From Bloomsbury to Calcutta

THE LITERARY history of the British Isles presents to American students an interesting phenomenon which is not often familiar to them in their own sprawling country: in almost every generation, back to Chaucer's day, we find writers grouped in circles, related by family and social ties as well as by intellectual interests, living together or in close neighbourhood, and forming cultural centres that transport, each time with a difference, the great tradition of English literature. In the twentieth century, the Bloomsbury Group is an obvious example.

J. K. Johnstone's book about them, published in 1954, laid an excellent foundation for the very numerous critical and biographical studies of Bloomsbury which have come out especially strong during the past ten years. Meanwhile, Bloomsbury's reputation has followed the typical pattern: attacks from enemies, retreat from public notice, neglect after the demise of some of the members, then a cautious revival of interest, then extravagances of appraisal, and now, just beginning to be discerned, a judicious and permanently based fame. Fortunately, at this same present time, literary criticism is returning to an appreciation of the influence that an author's life and social environment may have on his works; literature is beginning to be read again as the artful expression of human history.

E. M. Forster's image of the novel, for example, as a marshy territory watered equally by streams from the ranges of history and poetry, flowing through it to the eternal sea, may again be credited. He changed that image amusingly in his Rede lecture on Virginia Woolf; there he puts her as novelist up in a magical tree, like a singing bird, but then again like a monkey, holding on with one hand to the tree of poetry while stretching out the other to grasp bits of actual fact, which she then moulds and builds into the novel. Mrs. Woolf herself invented an image for the union of reality with vision in her admirable phrase 'granite and rainbow'.

My disposition as a student of literature has always been to know the authors themselves who are responsible for the works that I enjoy, and to understand the soil from which they sprang. With the Bloomsbury writers I was thus led to trace the connection between their families and some of the families in the Clapham Sect. Of course, I soon found that the limited coterie of Clapham in the late eighteenth and early nineteenth centuries expanded and ramified, their objects and outlines changing with the times and enlarged membership. Their interests from the beginning were in sharp contrast to those of Bloomsbury. But the few family connections with the Bloomsbury Group remained vital, and the tradition of intellectual and political interests continued. I recognized as I proceeded that the generation of Old Bloomsbury, born about 1880, and that of New Bloomsbury, born about 1910, were only recurrences in a series of distinguished generations of a handful of families. From the standpoint of those elders, twentieth-century Bloomsbury members might be viewed almost patronizingly, as merely living up in their own way to the family traditions of genius and talent, power and service, creation and distinction.

Rather early in that investigation, I began to be struck by the extraordinary women in these families. E. M. Forster's biography of his aunt, Marianne Thornton, confirmed my guess that among all these ancestors, the sisters and the mothers and the aunts, not to mention the cousins reckoned by the dozens, were people who had not been noticed as much as they deserved to be. There was the critical puzzle, first observed, I believe, by Lionel Trilling, of the recurring feminine character in Forster's novels—that sublime and enigmatic older woman, who dies, but leaves a presiding influence over the next generation. Another clue to the assertiveness of the female ancestors of Bloomsbury was the involvement of Lady Strachey and her relatives in the rise of the feminist movement in the 1860's. Then I stumbled across the legend of the Pattle sisters, who twenty years ago were not yet so famous as they are today, and had to pursue that story for its own amusement.

Gradually it appeared that I should narrow the field of

inquiry if I wanted to communicate to others the kinds of insight into Bloomsbury literature that I felt I was deriving from this study, for I had been rambling over the whole of British India in the company of Clapham adherents and Bloomsbury ancestors. It now seemed possible to hint at the whole enormous territory and its significance for understanding the Bloomsbury Group if I were to describe only a few of the mothers and aunts. These were interesting people in themselves and in their careers, who should not be forgotten. They also cropped up occasionally in one way or another as part of the 'granite' in Mrs. Woolf's fiction. Their influential power would help to explain the feminism, perhaps also the femininity, of the Bloomsbury Group members.

I have therefore concentrated on the Pattle sisters and on four other ladies, in a biographical sketch of each, attempting to provide something of their British and Anglo-Indian backgrounds and to suggest their relevance to Bloomsbury fiction or other Bloomsbury interests. I have arranged the chapters more or less chronologically, except that Julia Jackson Stephen naturally follows the Pattle sisters as their sequel. I am assuming that readers of this book are already acquainted with the Bloomsbury Group and its works, but if not, I would recommend as a brief, authoritative introduction Quentin Bell's *Bloomsbury* (1968).

I should confess that I am a sceptic, a scientifically illiterate sceptic, about the importance of genetic heredity in producing talented individuals, in spite of the fact that I appear to be implying it. I have asked myself whether there is any sense in digging into the family heritage of great writers for illumination on what they themselves thought and produced. Those members of Bloomsbury whom I had the privilege of knowing said yes, indeed, that is the way to understand them. The Stracheys were firm believers in the power of physical heredity to transmit intelligence and talent. They pointed with pride to their family's position in Francis Galton's pioneer book on *Hereditary Genius*. John Lehmann also argued with me the correctness of Paul Bloomfield's similar thesis in *Uncommon People*, a sort of sequel to Galton's work.

My own belief is that environmental, not genetic, influences play the major role in producing as well as developing talents.

In the case of Bloomsbury writers and artists, who lived not in any remote backwater but right at the centre of civilization, aware of every current, one must allow for far more than just family inheritance and upbringing in reckoning the sources of their qualities. Nevertheless, the family backgrounds and environments are primary and should not be ignored; in connection with Virginia Woolf, particularly so, since she tended to write everything for her immediate audience in the Bloomsbury Group, letting the public eavesdrop and make what they could of esoteric references.

As I have suggested, the Bloomsbury Group was relatively unknown territory to scholars when I started this study. By 1960, when it was taking shape, the reputation of Bloomsbury, in England especially, was at its lowest ebb, after a quarter century of decline. Recently, as it has surged up again, perhaps more for reasons of notoriety than for a true, lasting appreciation of its works, there has lingered a feeling of pathos, of misunderstanding, of injustice to departed glory, in the midst of the new attentions now being showered upon it. I remember once, when we had got to know each other well, Marjorie Strachey described herself and her sister Pippa, then in their eighties, as decayed gentlewomen sitting at home in 51 Gordon Square while their house collapsed slowly around them. True, the Duke of Bedford's Estate agency occasionally applied a fresh coat of paint to the stone front of the building, but inside there had been, I fear, no renovation for decades.

On my first visit, one rainy October afternoon, Pippa herself opened the heavy, black front door—it was the maid's afternoon out—letting me into the long, bare, unpainted hall, the walls of which were lined with fading photographs of the Victorian great. Marjorie led the way upstairs, moving rather briskly for one afflicted with arthritis, and disappeared into a kitchenette to make ready the tea, while Pippa guided me into the front drawing-room. It was furnished in the manner of a family of literary and scientific scholars—old leather-bound books to the ceiling at one end of the room, extremely well-worn chairs, tables draped in cloths and littered with handy debris, a small gas heater near my chair. On the grand piano stood the silver-framed profile photograph of Sir Richard Strachey, their famous father, and the walls bore many portraits of the family members, those of Lytton Strachey being familiar to me from reproductions.

We had scarcely seated ourselves, when Marjorie sang out from the rear, in the noted Strachey voice, 'PipPAH! I'm pouring!' Pippa trotted out to bring in the old-fashioned earthenware teapot, like one in my grandparents' home in Ohio. She insisted on waiting on me, her tremulous hands juggling full tea-cups and plates of chocolate cake, while Marjorie poured in awe-inspiring silence and stared me through and through, and I kept up a chatter of small talk. Eventually, it appeared that I had passed preliminary inspection. They kept me for over two hours in what amounted to an informal examination on Stracheys and Grants, their mother's family, the last questions including identification of the portraits in the hall on my way out. Pippa would point to a picture and ask me 'Who is that?' and crow with delight when I could say without prompting. One was of a cherubic young girl whom I did not recognize. 'That,' said she, 'is Janey'—i.e. Jane Bussy, their niece—'she has just died, and her mother Madame Bussy, our sister Dorothy, and our brother Oliver Strachey; they have also died, all within the past few months.'

The older Bloomsbury Group members who were still living in 1960–1 were well aware of the eclipse of their fame and were understandably mistrustful of an unknown American enthusiast such as I. Perhaps I was nothing but a gossipy skeleton-rattler. Pippa Strachey, in the presence of James and Marjorie one day, pressed me home about it. She got out of her little chair and came over to put her face down close to mine, so that with her almost sightless big brown eyes she might be able to read my expression. 'Why are you interested in our mother? Why are you interested in us?' Perhaps a century from now, I answered, the world would regard the Bloomsbury Group as another flowering of English culture at its best. The works of its members in journalism and politics, in criticism, economics, philosophy, science, and mathematics, even in painting and in promotion of the arts such as ballet and theatre—all these might be forgotten or absorbed into history, but there would be a half dozen or so of their books that would have survived and would still be treasured as classics. Scholars of the future would thank any researcher who ignored the then current trend of belittling Bloomsbury and helped to preserve its story for posterity.

The memoirs which follow are intended to be a small contribution to that end.

2

The Pattle Sisters

THE BLOOMSBURY GROUP developed from the early friendships of the young Stephens and Lytton Strachey and some of
their Cambridge friends. Vanessa and Virginia Stephen, though
they had not shared the university experience, were central to
the group because of their talents, their charm and beauty.
A goodly share of these attractions, no doubt, came from their
maternal inheritance, for they had as grandmother and great-
aunts, on their mother's side, a fabulous bevy of women known
to Victorian society as 'the famous Pattle sisters'. Adeline
Virginia Stephen (later Mrs. Woolf) was named for two of those
Pattle great-aunts. Victorian memoir writers assume, mistak-
enly, that their readers to this day will know all about them.
They were a legend in their own right, in the Victorian era,
and their story deserves retelling for the modern reader, even
regardless of their position as ancestresses of Bloomsbury.

There were seven Pattle sisters who lived to grow up, most
of them born in Calcutta. From eldest to youngest, they were:
Adeline Maria, born at Murshidabad, March 19, 1812; Julia
Margaret, born June 11, 1815; Sara Monckton, born August
16, 1816; Maria (nicknamed Mia), born at sea on July 7, 1818;
Louisa Colebrooke, born October 5, 1821; Virginia, born
January 14, 1827; and Sophia Ricketts, born March 19, 1829.

Legend has it that six of the seven Pattle sisters were very
beautiful and the seventh plain but talented. Legend, as usual,
exaggerates; two—Maria and Virginia—were indeed very
beautiful; four ranged from pretty to 'comely'; and one, Julia,
was 'actually plain'.

About their father, James Pattle (1775–1845), the facts are few
and dry (see Appendix A), but the rumours, if not luxuriant,
are at least succulent. His great-granddaughter, Virginia Woolf,
appears to have accepted the gossip, for she wrote that Jim
Pattle 'was a gentleman of marked, but doubtful, reputation,
who after living a riotous life and earning the title of "the

biggest liar in India", finally drank himself to death. . . .' Some
doubt has been cast upon this gossip, however, by the possibility
that it may refer not to James Pattle, but to his brother, Col.
William Pattle.

James Pattle's career in the Bengal Civil Service began in
1791, when he was but sixteen years old; it was soon interrupted
for some unexplained return to England, and resumed without
loss of rank by an extraordinary permission of the Court of
Proprietors of the Honourable East India Company in 1795, at
the time of his father's resignation as a Director of the Company.
The Court observed that 'Mr. [James] Pattle was a man the
most capable of any to render the Company great and essential
service, and one whose merits claimed every regard from their
hands.' Some political horse-trading may be suspected in these
manoeuvres involving parent and son. Anyway, young Pattle
is next seen in 1800 residing with his parents at Murshidabad
on the Ganges, as Register to the provincial court, with the
rank of Factor. From there, through promotions to various
district judgeships, he was drawn into the centre of things at
Calcutta.

On February 18, 1811, at Bhagulpur, James Pattle had
married Adeline de l'Etang, eldest daughter of a couple of ro-
mantically interesting French émigrés, from whom were derived
the good looks and ebullient temperament of the Pattle sisters
and their descendants (see Appendix B). In Calcutta, Mr. and
Mrs. James Pattle lived for a time in Garden Reach, then the
favourite suburb, but moved to a house in Chowringhee when
that quarter became the more fashionable. By 1821 Pattle had
found a berth on the Western Board of the Sudder Board of
Revenue. His eldest brother Thomas Jr.'s death in 1815, and his
father's death in 1818, with the consequent inheritance of wealth,
must have smoothed his path, for James Pattle's name begins to
appear in 1822 in the *Calcutta Gazette* as one of the substantial
citizens in public affairs. Twenty years later, in 1842, he was
not only the senior member of the Board of Revenue, with a
salary of 4,583 rupees a month, but also the oldest active member
of the whole Bengal Civil Service. *The Bengal Obituary*, on the
melancholy occasion of his death, says 'he lived respected and
beloved'. He had at least tenacity and a very hardy liver.
William Tayler, of Sepoy Mutiny fame, testifies that Mr. Pattle

was a kindly *bon vivant*, who served 'tip-top champagne' at his dinner-parties and looked out benevolently for the welfare of junior civil servants.

The final public-spirited enterprise of James Pattle commemorated in print does suggest that he was strongly interested in long cold drinks, for in 1833 he served on a committee with Sir Edward Ryan and James Prinsep to see to the construction of the Calcutta Ice House, wherein was to be stored the ice that Mr. Frederick Tudor, of Boston, Massachusetts, was planning to import. The day the first cargo of ice from America reached Calcutta was a red-letter day. Without provision for refrigerating it, the cargo had to be used up as fast as possible. 'All business was suspended until noon. . . . Everybody invited everybody to dinner, to taste of claret and beer cooled by the American importation. . . .'

Another rumour relates that Mr. Pattle was popularly known as Jemmy Blazes, though his brother, Col. William Pattle, seems to have shared this nickname and a fondness for long drinks and tall stories (see Appendix C). Some of the dashing nature of Mr. Pattle's daughters must have been derived from their father as well as from their maternal ancestors.

Their mother, Adeline de l'Etang Pattle (1793–1845), was said to have inherited her mother's grace and beauty. She brought up her seven daughters, aided doubtless by a small army of Indian ayahs, and this involved frequent journeys to the Cape of Good Hope, to England and to Paris, in search of a more healthful climate and better educational opportunities. The gossip was that her husband ill-treated her, and it is not hard to imagine Jim Pattle, an Anglo-Indian of the old school, surrounded by his bevy of women folk more French than English, delighting in teasing them. Perhaps there is a shade of irony in the Scripture text chosen by his children for his memorial tablet in St. John's Church, Calcutta: 'O be Thou our help in trouble, for vain is the help of man.' The memorial goes on, 'Sacred to the memory of . . . Adeline, his Wife . . . "And all wept and bewailed her. . . ."'

The object of the girls' education was of course to fit them for brilliant marriages, and to this end, after they had had a few years' schooling in England, Mrs. Pattle placed them with her mother at Versailles for a French finishing in the mode of

Madame Campan, at whose school Mrs. Pattle had been a
pupil in the Napoleonic era. Madame de l'Etang taught the
girls 'all sorts of housewifely arts'—dressmaking, cookery,
home nursing, and the arts of entertaining.

In Paris and Versailles, where Mrs. Pattle stayed for prolonged visits with her mother and her two sisters, Mrs. Impey
and Mrs. Beadle, the Thackerays, the Ritchies, and other
Anglo-Indians made the acquaintance of the girls as they began
to enter society. W. M. Thackeray, who had tried in vain to
find Mrs. Pattle at home in London during the spring of 1832,
while she was busy with her eldest daughter's wedding, called
on the Impeys in Paris that October and met her there. Then
on two occasions he spent a happy day with her, her sister Mrs.
Beadle, and Madame de l'Etang at Versailles, and the following
autumn, again in Paris, he made a custom of spending evenings
with Mrs. Pattle. Apparently she went so far as to suggest that
he marry one of her daughters, probably Julia as the next in
line for matrimony. But nothing came of it, for Thackeray had
just lost his inheritance in the Calcutta bank failures, and Mrs.
Pattle appears therefore to have lost interest in him as an
eligible match.

With the exception of the two youngest girls, all the Pattles
were married off during the 1830's. At that time there was still a
dearth of eligible English brides in Calcutta. At a Government
House dinner party in 1829, 'each lady was handed in by two
gentlemen', a custom 'indicating a great plethora of the male
sex in Calcutta'. The Hon. Emily Eden, a few years later, trying
to get up a quadrille, found the number of young women dancing partners in all the city to stop short at sixteen. As husbands,
civil servants were always preferred to the military because of
their greater prospects for advancement and wealth and their
greater stability of life.

In such a fertile field, the Pattle sisters, all more or less
beautiful and interesting, made a sensational success. 'None of
the Pattles suffered from the "inferiority complex", as it would
be called now. Everything they did, said and thought mat-
tered, according to them, . . . with their superabundant energy,
their untempered enthusiasms, their strangle-hold on life, their
passionate loves and hates.' So Lady Troubridge, one of their
descendants, remembered them in their later years; what must

they have been like as teenage girls? Besides there were so
many of them. As one observer put it, remembering his visit
to India in 1850-1, when he sat next to Julia's husband in the
ship's dining saloon, and met Sophia's husband at Madras,
'You must know that wherever you go in India you meet with
some member of this family. Every other man has married,
and every other woman has been, a Miss Pattle.'

Adeline, 'then barely eighteen', met her fate on board ship in
March 1830, sailing with her parents and two youngest sisters
from Calcutta to the Cape. Among their fellow-passengers
was twenty-four-year-old Lieut. Colin Mackenzie, 'of a junior
branch of the Redcastle Mackenzies', on sick leave from the
48th Madras Native Infantry to recover from jungle fever. She
fell in love with this 'blond Adonis', who had already had five
years' duelling, tiger-hunting, and marching through back
country. A year or so later, in England, Mackenzie renewed the
shipboard friendship, and Adeline and he were married in
London in May 1832. But their married life was brief. Back in
India, Adeline fell ill while visiting her parents and sisters in
Calcutta; Mackenzie was absent with his regiment on guard
duty in the Straits of Malacca. Shortly after he had rejoined her,
she was forced to sail for Europe 'if her life was to be saved'. On
shipboard she died on her wedding anniversary, May 26, 1836,
and was buried at sea. She left three small daughters.

With the early death of Adeline, Julia became the eldest
Pattle sister. She had returned to Calcutta from Paris in 1834,
with Sara, Maria, Louisa, and their mother. On February 1,
1838, she married, as his second wife, Charles Hay Cameron, the
distinguished Benthamite jurist, whom she had met at the Cape
a year or two earlier. He was forty-three and she twenty-three
years old. Cameron had been sent to Bengal in 1835 as legal
representative from England to the new law commission for the
Supreme Council of India, where he continued Macaulay's
work on the penal code and shared his views and efforts to
reform Indian education. By 1843, Cameron was appointed the
first legal Member of Council, a position in which according to
protocol he and his wife outranked socially almost everyone else
in British India. During the next five years, when under
Ellenborough and Dalhousie there happened to be no governor-
general's lady in Calcutta to lead society, that pleasant duty

devolved upon Julia Pattle Cameron, and she enjoyed it to the fullest extent. There were the usual Government House receptions, balls, and dinners. There was the Cricket Club, that Cameron had started with Sir Edward Ryan. There were also literary pursuits—verse-writing, translating, and literary conversazione. The Camerons' home was noted for its hospitality and witty conversation. And there was the great drive that Julia Cameron conducted to raise £10,000 for Irish famine relief.

Sara Pattle, though a year younger, had beaten Julia to the altar, when she married on May 14, 1835, Henry Thoby Prinsep, also twenty years her senior, and newly appointed Member of Council. Prinsep came from an exalted Anglo-Indian family and had already made a name for himself as a member of the government secretariat in charge of legal affairs, and as a writer and Persian scholar. At the end of 1843, shortly after Cameron came on the Supreme Council, Thoby Prinsep resigned his seat, and also his presidency of the Calcutta Asiatic Society, and he and his wife returned to live in London.

Maria Pattle married in Calcutta, January 17, 1837, Dr. John Jackson, who had been appointed Assistant Surgeon, under 'civil employ', to the Hon. E. I. Co. in 1830. Dr. Jackson was on the staff of the Bengal Presidency General Hospital in Calcutta, and in 1841 was appointed professor at the recently organized Medical College. He held office on the committee of management of the Bengal Medical Retiring Fund, and also in the Medical and Physical Society of Calcutta, before which he read papers on surgical operations, cardiac cases, and diseases of the liver. In short, his career was marked with distinguished service; Gerald Ritchie, writing as late as 1920, says, 'The name of Dr. Jackson is still affectionately remembered and quoted by the Indians in Calcutta.' Maria and her husband, as respected members of the Calcutta community, did not however cut so large a figure in its British society as her sisters Julia and Sara and their husbands.

Louisa Pattle, the fifth in line of seniority, was married in Calcutta on December 6, 1838, to Henry Vincent Bayley, eldest son of the distinguished Judge William Butterworth Bayley, who had recently returned to London as a Director of the Company. Henry, named after his uncle who was a well-known Cambridge scholar, is somewhat overshadowed in official records by the fame of his younger brother Sir Steuart Colvin Bayley. Nevertheless, he had a sound career in the Bengal Civil Service, to which he had been appointed in 1834. The young William Taylers got acquainted with the Henry Bayleys in 1843 in Midnapore, a few miles west of Calcutta, where Henry was Collector and William was Judge for a time. They visited each other's houses, nursed each other's children through illnesses, shared a month's vacation at the Calcutta seaside resort with the interesting name of Beercool, and in October 1843 enjoyed a weekend house-party at the Taylers', to which came Mrs. James Pattle and her two unmarried daughters, Virginia and Sophia (recently returned from Paris), the Charles Prinseps, and other friends from Calcutta. The house-party diverted itself in the evenings with charades and tableaux, the Pattle girls serving as statues in Pygmalion's studio, and as hay-makers in the second syllable of the word *defamation*. Henry Bayley's Midnapore appointment ended with a furlough in 1849, and he returned to England for a while, whither Louisa and their children had preceded him some years before.

While their older sisters were getting married in Calcutta, Virginia and Sophia had been finishing their education with their grandmother at Versailles. Thackeray met them in 1839, crossing to England with their aunt Mrs. Beadle, and reported them to be 'prettier than their sisters: all the others, 4, are married and multiplying vastly Mrs. B. says: and she adds that Mrs. P. is adored by her sons-in-law. There's a wonder for you!' The girls went back to Calcutta with their mother in the autumn of 1842; William Ritchie wrote his sister of meeting them: 'Do you remember Mrs. Pattle, in Paris, about ten years since? The two youngest daughters . . . are two of the prettiest and nicest girls [in Calcutta]. The old lady herself [Mrs. Pattle was then fifty-one] is still looking [illegible] and desired me at a ball the other night at her daughter's, Mrs. Cameron's, to remember her kindly to my mother, if she recollected her, and to give her love to William Thackeray.'

But before the two youngest daughters can be disposed of in matrimony, it becomes a melancholy duty to record the deaths of Mr. and Mrs. James Pattle. Mr. Pattle died 'at his residence in Chowringhee, on Thursday the 4th of September, 1845, in

the 69th year of his age. . . . He had been suffering for a long
period from a painful disease. . . .' Whether he 'drank himself
to death' seems debatable. Nevertheless, there remains an aura
of spirits—if not of claret, champagne, and brandy-pawnee, at
least of rum—surrounding his memory, owing to the circumstances of his burial. In the days before refrigeration, it was
sometimes customary for one who died abroad and wished to be
interred at home to have his body preserved in a cask of rum
for the long voyage over the 'black water'. This according to
contemporary evidence was Mr. Pattle's earnest wish, and 'his
remains were sent to England and deposited in the Vault of his
family at Camberwell'. But somehow a legend grew, until we
find in the twentieth century two versions of disaster.

The earlier and more lurid was delivered by Gen. J. H. Smyth
at a Christmas house-party in 1890, recorded at the time by his
daughter, Dame Ethel Smyth, and published in her *Impressions
That Remained* (1919), from which Mrs. Woolf gleefully quoted
it in introducing her great-aunt Julia's photographs. The other
comes from E. F. Benson's *As We Were* (the Bensons and
Smyths were great friends), and reads as follows: Mr. Pattle
'died out in India, and since he had expressed his wish to be
buried in England, his widow procured a large barrel into which
the deceased was folded, and the barrel was then filled up to
the top with some reliable preservative, rum or Pondicherry
liquor, something with body in it, in two senses of the word.
The widow then travelled back to England where her daughters
awaited her, on the ship which conveyed the remains. . . . Off
the Cape of Good Hope the vessel encountered so violent a buf-
feting from a storm, that Mr Pattle's barrel broke from its moor-
ings and rolled about with a very dreadful liveliness. Before
it could be bridled again, a violent collision with the ship's
side broached it, smashing off the top and spilling such contents
as were liquid; what was solid peered starkly over the battered
staves. There was not enough liquor on the ship nor a large
enough barrel to make possible any further homing of the
contents, and after the widow had formally identified them
they were buried at sea. Before the ship reached England
Mr Pattle's widow also died and his large fortune descended to
his daughters.'

General Smyth's version, which pretends to be first-hand,

says that the catastrophe occurred before the ship even left the
mouth of the Hooghly River. The cask containing the corpse
'ready to be shipped off to England . . . [was] placed in a spare
room next [the widow's] bedroom till the vessel was ready to
carry him off. Well, in the middle of the night there was a
loud explosion; she rushed into the room and found the cask
had burst—and there was her husband half out of it! The shock
sent her off her head then and there, poor thing, and she died
raving. . . . All the same his friends thought they'd better carry
out his wishes, so they had him put up again and taken down
the Ganges. The sailors hadn't the most distant idea what they'd
got on board, and thinking the cask was full of rum, which was
the case, they tapped it and got drunk; and, by Jove, the rum
ran out and got alight and set the ship on fire! And while they
were trying to extinguish the flames she ran on a rock, blew up,
and drifted ashore just below Hooghly. And what do you think
the sailors said?—that Pattle had been such a scamp that the
Devil wouldn't let him go out of India.' Short of an order from
the Home Secretary to inspect the contents of the Pattle family
vault, or indeed that great day when the sea shall give up its
dead, it is unlikely that this conflicting evidence will ever be
straightened out. However, there is no disagreement about the
fact of Mrs. Pattle's death and burial at sea, '11th Nov. 1845,
aged 52'.

Probably as many of James Pattle's daughters as were able
to leave Calcutta had accompanied their mother on this fatal
voyage, and remained in England either with their sister Sara
in London, or in lodgings at Brighton. Thackeray wrote his
mother from London, March 6, 1846, very soon after their
arrival, 'I am going to day to dine with the Prinseps and all the
Pattle girls.' At least Virginia and Sophia made the voyage to
the East again, to stay with the Camerons in all their splendour,
for Sophia was married in Calcutta on June 7, 1847, to John
Warrender Dalrymple, B.C.S. But again according to Thackeray, Louisa Bayley was in Brighton in 1847, for he wrote to his
brother-in-law, November 15: 'One of my prettiest and amia-
blest female friends Mrs. Henry Bayley has just fallen at Brighton
where the F. C [i.e. Thackeray himself, the Fat Contributor to
Punch] used to ride with her, and broken her nose—the dearest
little nose in the world. . . . Mrs. Bayley sent me a bottle of

chutney—I wish you could have seen her face when I told her that I was very much obliged to her & had rubbed it into my hair.' Again the next year he alludes occasionally to visits with various Pattle sisters, especially to the 'lovely VIRGINIA'. In fact by 1848, when the Camerons, who had retired, and Maria Jackson and her three daughters had all come home, the scene of action for the Pattle sisters had shifted from India to England, except for a poor stray husband now and then, and the curtain was about to go up on what was known as 'Pattledom'.

The H. T. Prinseps had had several years' headstart in London Society. With their three boys and one girl, Alice (who later married Charles Gurney of Gurney's Bank), and a great many uncles, aunts, and cousins, they formed a large Victorian tribe, which served as a nucleus for the rest of the family. Augusta Prinsep Becher recalls an extraordinary 'coming out' party for her cousin Caroline Haldimand on Twelfth Day, 1845, when all the members of the Prinsep family, even to the ninety-year-old grandmother, Mrs. John Prinsep, were gathered in the artificially darkened dining-room at Uncle George Haldimand's in Belgrave Square for a three o'clock dinner: 'Such a dinner; trees on the table covered with real oranges . . . ; a pudding which flew up to the ceiling when the cover was taken off; a pie, out of which jumped a jack-in-the-box when it was cut. Everything lovely, with jolly, noisy, merry Uncles Thoby and William, and grandmama carefully enthroned at the head of the table, and all the cousins down to Arthur, then the youngest [third son of Thoby and Sara Prinsep]—twenty-eight of us. All had lovely presents delivered to us by Uncle William in postman's costume. All had money in their presents—from £50 to the eldest, Willie, to £ to baby Arthur. Mine was £5. Only Carry had no money, but a most splendid bracelet. At dinner and at supper the tables were quite covered with lovely cases and boxes of every device, full of bon-bons, of which we were to take all we liked! Then there was a bran-pie full of toys, a conjuror, a dwarf, and I don't know what all. . . . This was to us, a sort of Arabian Night's entertainment, and its memory lasted long.'

Thoby Prinsep, genial and generous with his family and friends, was in his official life stubbornly independent and 'a conservative to the backbone'. In Calcutta, he and his brother James had been leaders of the opposition in the question of educational reform; over this issue H. T. Prinsep and Macaulay 'butted one another like two bulls'. He differed with both Bentinck and Auckland over other policies; Miss Eden called him '*the* Prinsep . . . the greatest bore Providence ever created, and so contradictory that he will not let anybody agree or differ with him'. In London, as a Member of Parliament and a Director of the East India Company (eventually on the new Council of India), he continued his severe and authoritative scrutiny of Indian affairs. But in private life, he was a friend and Maecenas to artists—'large and philosophic in mind, grand in his stature, his learning, his memory, his everything, even to his sneeze! (once received with an *encore* from the gallery of a theatre), childlike in his gentleness and in the sweetness of his nature. . . .' He made up in balance for what his wife lacked, since with her 'restless energy . . . she was the kind of woman who would have turned a convent into a scene of tumult'.

With the help of the painter, G. F. Watts, who had got acquainted with them the year before, Thoby and Sara Prinsep moved into Little Holland House in the autumn of 1850, and settled down to a brilliant social career. Watts, whom Sara had been nursing through his frequent migraine headaches 'with her genius for all sorts of confections', soon moved in with them. As Sara put it, 'he came to stay three days, he stayed thirty years'. With her two men as drawing cards, Sara's Sunday afternoons at home became famous, in the summertime beauty of the old Holland House estate, 'only two miles from Hyde Park Corner, with much untouched country still around it. . . . When the garden emptied, and tea and the games of croquet or bowls were at an end,' and all the strawberries and cream had been consumed, 'the big crimson sofas and seats . . . were carried in,' and an 'impromptu dinner-party followed. The evenings were filled up, either by music or by much delightful conversation. . . .'

Among the frequent visitors, besides the members of this large family, were old Indian friends—the Thackerays, Herschels, Edward Ryans, and Hardinges—and many new friends, Henry Taylor and his wife, the Tennysons, the Kemble family, especially Adelaide Sartoris and her husband, Ruskin, Browning, Rossetti, Burne-Jones, Leighton, Mrs. Norton,

Coutts Lindsay, 'Jacob Omnium' (i.e. Matthew James Higgins), Tom Taylor, Richard Doyle, Tom Hughes, his brothers and his sister, Mrs. Nassau Senior—'women remarkable for gifts of talent and beauty . . . as well as statesmen, soldiers, painters, poets. . . .' In the garden of Little Holland House, Sir John Herschel 'first saw the great comet of 1857. . . .' Dicky Doyle, who always spent Christmas with the Prinseps, once met Tennyson there and waited eagerly for the verbal music he expected when the great poet should speak, but was rewarded with Tennyson's remark: 'Legs of mutton should be cut in wedges.' After dinner, in the drawing-room with the blue ceiling decorated with silver and gold stars, and the walls lined with paintings, Joachim played his violin and Mrs. Sartoris sang Tennyson's songs to him. For a while Ellen and Kate Terry were also inmates of Little Holland House, until Sara's well-meant matchmaking between Ellen and Watts 'went astray. . . . Dear Ellen herself speaks of [Sara's] kindness, and I am sure that seeing these beautiful young women, Ellen and Kate, her affectionate admiration for them knew no bounds, and she wanted to gather them under her wing and adopt them as she adopted half the world. . . .'

Meanwhile, Julia Cameron, always Sara's closest crony and rival among the sisters, was setting herself to create a complementary salon. She and her family had all assembled in England, when Cameron had retired from the government in Calcutta early in 1848, to devote himself to his classical studies and live on the proceeds of his coffee plantations in Ceylon. At first the Camerons lived in Tunbridge Wells, where they made lifelong friends of the Henry Taylors, and then they moved to East Sheen near London, to be near the Taylors and the Prinsep circle. Three of the five Cameron boys were at school, and the other two at home with their parents, their one sister, Julia, and occasionally visiting cousins.

Thackeray took his daughters Anny and Minny one summer's day to Sheen to see his old friend Mrs. Cameron. 'My father,' Lady Ritchie writes, 'who had known [Julia] first as a girl in Paris, laughed and said: "She is quite unchanged," . . . generous, unconventional, loyal and unexpected.' She offered to write for him, but Thackeray declined the honour. Watts painted Julia's portrait about 1852, a somewhat idealized picture showing 'a woman of noble plainness carrying herself with dignity and expression, and well able to set off the laces and Indian shawls she wore so carelessly'. In that same year began the Camerons' acquaintance with the Tennysons, which ripened into a devoted friendship. From Sheen the Camerons moved to Putney Heath, some time after 1852, where they remained for several years. The older boys finished their schooling and went out to Ceylon, where Mr. Cameron also made occasional visits. The daughter was brought out, engaged and married to Charles Norman in 1859, and settled at Bromley.

At the Little Holland House parties, Julia Cameron was in her element. Her fine dark eyes flashed like her wit. Her love of poetry extended far beyond the poems—which she read aloud with fine expression—to the poets who created them. There was no limit to the breadth and depth of her affections. After she had taken up photography, she would range about the lawn and gardens among the groups of happy visitors, singling out with an irresistible compulsion important visitors to be 'immortalized' by her camera. Her generosity was boundless, overflowing in letters and gifts, unsolicited medical advice, Christmas boxes, a prayer-book for Carlyle, a frill for Mrs. Tennyson, a 'coatee' and 'beautiful big ball' for little Hallam, prints of her photographs, worth a guinea apiece, and whole albums of them for her special favourites.

Nor were she and Sara left out of other people's at homes. Anny Thackeray, at seventeen just venturing into society, met them at Mrs. Brookfield's one evening with Miss Mildmay, the Sterlings, Mr. Maurice, and many more, and the next day, 'we dined at Little Holland House, where we met Tom Taylor and had a pleasant party'. One day Anny and Mrs. Cameron went together to hear Mr. Brookfield preach, at some London chapel. 'Mrs. Cameron led the way into the gallery and took up her place in front exactly facing the pulpit. When Mr. Brookfield appeared climbing the pulpit stairs to deliver his sermon, his head was so near us that we could have almost touched it. Mrs. Cameron chose this moment to lean forward and kiss her hand to him repeatedly. Poor Mr. Brookfield sank suddenly down upon his knees and buried his face in the pulpit cushion.' A long letter from Julia Cameron to Tennyson shows that the Camerons were part of a very large house-party in 1855 at Sir

Ivor and Lady Charlotte Guest's. With every new acquaintance, Julia made a conquest; yet she and her sisters were never accused of tuft-hunting, though sometimes recipients of their warm-hearted, large-gesturing affection felt somewhat oppressed. Sir Henry Taylor referred to them and their artistic and hospitable activities under the generic term of Pattledom, or more privately, as 'Watts' "Holy Family" '.

In 1860, Mr. Cameron, having recovered from an illness—miraculously in view of the terrifying ministrations of Julia's nursing—went on another trip to Ceylon, and Julia was left for the first time very nearly alone. Encouraged by the Tennysons, whom she went to visit at Farringford Hall, and without consulting her husband, she decided to move to the Isle of Wight, 'purchasing a couple of cottages that stood half way between Farringford and the sea', and 'had them joined together by building a tower in between'. Letters between Emily Tennyson and Julia became more frequent, as the Tennysons helped with the 'lawyers, business agents, purchases, furnishings', and loaned the services of their gardener for landscaping the grounds. 'Yes,' wrote Julia, 'how dear it will be for our children to grow and live happily together playing mad pranks along the healthy lea.'

Now began the palmy days for Julia Cameron, her friends and family, at 'Dimbola', as they called the new house near Freshwater Bay. Wilfrid Ward is emphatic about the quality of the social life enjoyed there and about Mrs. Cameron's responsibility in helping to create it. 'The Freshwater society,' he writes, 'of which Tennyson was the centre in the 'sixties and 'seventies approached, I think, nearer to realizing the purpose and ideal of a French *salon* than any social group I have myself known in England. . . . Mrs. Cameron had . . . much to do with forming [it]. . . . Her keen, eager spirit created by its natural force a world of incident and interest. . . .' The Wards and the Simeons lived nearby and were frequent visitors. Besides the little theatre for the plays put on by the young people and coached by Julia Cameron, she also built a special cottage for Professor Jowett (whom she called 'little Benjamin their ruler'), where he could bring his students for the long vacations. The Taylors visited Dimbola spring and autumn, a fortnight at a time. After Thackeray's death, his daughters were tenants of the little cottage called The Porch, where Mrs. Jeanie Hughes Senior also stayed. The Charles Darwins came for a summer vacation in 1868. Tourists—American and Continental, exalted and humble—and officers from the fort drifted in and out. If people did not come to visit the Camerons, they stayed with the Tennysons. Charades, walks and picnics, dances and dinner-parties, and informal visiting from house to house at all times of day and night made life a constant holiday.

The stories of Julia Cameron's impulsive behaviour are so numerous that there is space here to record only a few representative ones. Wilfrid Ward gives the best version of the one concerning Tennyson's vaccination: 'Mrs. Cameron was profoundly interested in keeping the poet well, and fit for work. One evening a friend who was dining with her mentioned that there was small-pox in the neighbourhood. Mrs. Cameron started. "Alfred Tennyson has not been vaccinated for twenty years," she said. "We must not lose a moment." She went at once in search of the village doctor, took him to Farringford, and made her way to Tennyson's study. He was busy and did not want to see her, but she pursued him from room to room [other versions say he finally took refuge in a tower where she hammered on the door, calling him 'Coward, coward!']. In the end, he said: "Madam, if you will leave me I will do anything you like." He was vaccinated. The sequel was told me by Tennyson himself. The vaccine proved to be bad, and he was not really well again for six months.' But Tennyson loved Julia Cameron and her 'wild-beaming benevolence', as he called it; she was almost his only woman friend whom he called by her first name.

Many of the stories about Julia concern her photography, the absorbing pursuit she began in 1863, after the Normans had given her a photographic outfit. She was like one possessed, a tyrant to herself and her sitters. Lady Troubridge's first recollection of her great-aunt Julia was in this wise: 'To me, I frankly own, she appeared as a terrifying elderly woman, short and squat, with none of the Pattle grace and beauty about her . . . dressed in dark clothes, stained with chemicals from her photography (and smelling of them, too), with a plump, eager face and piercing eyes and voice husky, and a little harsh, yet in some way compelling and even charming. . . . Immediately

we, Rachel and I, were pressed into the service of the camera.
Our *rôles* were no less than those of two angels of the Nativity,
and to sustain them we were scantily clad, and each had a pair
of heavy swan's wings fastened to her narrow shoulders, while
Aunt Julia, with ungentle hand, touzled our hair to get rid of
its nursery look.

'No wonder those old photographs of us, leaning over imaginary ramparts of heaven, look anxious and wistful. This is how
we felt, for we never knew what Aunt Julia was going to do next,
nor did any one else for the matter of that. All we were conscious
of was that once in her clutches, we were perfectly helpless.
'Stand there,' she shouted. And we stood for hours, if necessary,
gazing at the model of the Heavenly Babe (in reality a sleeping
child deposited in a property manger). The parents, anxious
and uneasy, were outside, no more able to rescue their infant
until Aunt Julia had finished with it, than we should have been.'

Next to Sir Henry Taylor and her relatives, Tennyson was
Julia's favourite photographic subject, but a reluctant one. He
said she made bags under his eyes, and had rendered his
countenance so recognizable that he was charged double
wherever he went. To save himself from being victimized too
often, he fed her his guests. 'When he brought Longfellow . . . he
said "Longfellow, you will have to do whatever she tells you.
I will come back soon and see what is left of you." '

Mrs. Cameron's maids, chosen for their beauty, helped her as
models, photographic assistants, and errand-runners to fetch in
those passing strangers whose looks struck her as photogenic.
She would break off suddenly, as she did one day in conversation
with the friend who relates this tale, and 'rushing away at full
speed with extended arms,' called out, ' "Stop him, stop him;
there goes Time." ' And the shirtless old peasant, having been
captured and given a very necessary washing, would be decked
'in her best shawls, and duly photographed' as old Father Time.
Among the parlourmaids 'there were two "Marys" whom she
would sometimes in the most unconventional way take with
her into society. On one occasion when the Simeons asked her
to come to the Cowes regatta, somewhat to their surprise the
Marys appeared in her train. But the result was most embarras-
sing to Mrs. Cameron, as some of the more susceptible young
men of the party paid them attentions which made the duties

of a chaperon very onerous.' Mr. Cameron, white-haired and picturesque in his oriental dress, when badgered too often by his wife to pose for her, retreated to an upper room. She would take visitors to look in on him. 'One went on tiptoe to the door of his study, a crack of which was opened noiselessly: "There he is, reading his Greek; doesn't he look grand?" '

Although Mrs. Cameron photographed with primitive materials and equipment (the hens were dispossessed to make a studio out of the henhouse, the coal-shed became her dark-room, and she herself pumped nine buckets of water from the well to run over each negative), her hobby ran into money. Darwin was apparently the only sitter from whom she ever accepted payment, though the Tennysons tried to reimburse her for expenses. Once she read 'a notice about the recovery of silver from photographic solutions', and impulsively rushed off to London, with her waste solutions in bottles, to find out how to reclaim the metal, only to learn that she had spent more on the trip than all the silver would be worth. Exhibitions of her work, from the spring of 1864 on, in London, Dublin, Berlin, and other continental cities, made her pictures well known and helped the sale of prints, which to Victorian collectors had come to rival engravings. In 1874, Tennyson suggested that she make a set of photographs to illustrate his *Idylls of the King*, which was about to be republished in The People's Edition; but when the volume appeared, she was so much disappointed, the publisher having reduced her pictures to very small woodcuts, that she had the illustrations published separately, in January 1875, together with the passages they alluded to, copied out in her own handwriting. Subsequently she published another volume of twelve more illustrations for the *Idylls and Other Poems*. 'I hope,' she wrote to Sir Edward Ryan, soliciting his aid in having the first volume reviewed, 'to get one single grain of the momentous mountain heap of profits the poetical part of the work brings in to Alfred.'

These illustrations are not at all Mrs. Cameron's best work—her lasting fame is owing to her portraits of the Victorian great—but they are certainly the most amusing and most revealing of her odd nature. Not for nothing had Julia Cameron indulged in the favourite entertainment of Pattledom, and indeed of most Victorian society—charades and tableaux—for that is what these pictures are. She had trouble getting exactly the models she wanted. Ward's story has often been repeated, about the myopic Tennyson's remark when Julia pointed out the saintly Cardinal Vaughan as a suitable model for Launcelot —'I want a face that is well worn with evil passion.' Tennyson liked best her pictures of the porter from the Yarmouth pier as King Arthur. Guineveres and Vivians were hard to come by. Any young summer visitors were pressed into service to pose for the scores of plates Julia ruined before she got the effects she wanted. One of these girls has left a report of the fatiguing job she had 'lying on the floor for . . . two hours, clutching the porter's ankle' to illustrate these lines from *Guinevere*:

> He paused, and in the pause she crept an inch
> Nearer, and laid her hands about his feet. . . .

The illustration of Merlin and Vivian was very hard to do, chiefly because Mr. Cameron, who had to pose for Merlin, was given to fits of laughter when he was supposed to be looking drowsy and charmed. A hollow oak from Tennyson's grounds was removed to the studio for him to pose inside; and it was always too much for the Vivian's composure when the oak would begin to shiver and shake with his suppressed chuckling. When the plate had been developed, 'Merlin had moved too much, there were at least fifty Merlins to be seen.' For the passing of Arthur, the stately barge was represented by an ordinary rowboat, lugged into the glass-house. The Yarmouth porter as Arthur lies uncomfortably on the thwarts, 'the boat is too small to contain the three mourning Queens, two of whom have to stand behind it. . . . Mr Cameron, in a monk's dark cowl, sits in the stern holding an oar with which he rows in the imaginary water, represented by white muslin curtains. . . . The background cloth does not stretch far enough, and reveals odd corners and part of the roof' of the henhouse.

In commenting on Mrs. Cameron's debt to the Pre-Raphaelite painters and Watts, Gernsheim notes that though she did not share their enthusiasm for meticulous detail, she was touched by the same cult for beauty and fondness for allegory and myth: 'She is more akin to Dante Gabriel Rossetti in sentiment than to any other painter of this movement. Many of her beautiful women have the strange emotional quality and melancholy expression which we find so often in Rossetti's faces, but in contrast to his voluptuous types, Mrs. Cameron always chose "nice young girls", whom she draped in robes of virgin whiteness, with their long hair flowing loosely. [These were, of course, the Pattle daughters and granddaughters and their friends.] Though the virginity is beyond question (Mrs. Prinsep told her nieces always to read their Bibles before going to dances, to give them "heavenly expressions"), the melancholy had sometimes to be artificially induced. . . . For the picture called "Despair" she locked up the unfortunate girl for two hours because she did not look sad enough for her idea of despair. . . . The Pre-Raphaelites failed because they became photographers in painting, and Mrs. Cameron, . . . and a host of other Victorian photographers, failed because they were painters in photography. . . .'

The high tide of Freshwater society was reached in 1874–5, when the circle was enlarged by the addition of the Thoby Prinsep household. Simultaneously with Mr. Prinsep's approaching retirement, Lady Holland decided in 1871 that she must sell Little Holland House and its grounds to make room for a new housing development. This was a shock to Watts and the Prinseps who had expected to live the rest of their lives there. Watts redoubled his efforts to make money, taking on quantities of portraiture for quick returns, and with the money, at Tennyson's suggestion, bought property adjoining Farringford and had a charming three-storey house built on it, which he gave to the Prinseps. This was a noble requital for the many years he had passed as a member of their household. The family did not settle in at Freshwater until the spring of 1874; from then until Mr. Prinsep's death in 1878, that corner of the Isle of Wight was at the height of its social bloom.

The Prinsep household at the 'Briary' in Freshwater was large and frequently augmented by visitors. Watts was with them much of the time. So were Sophie Pattle Dalrymple, and an assortment of granddaughters, nieces, and grandnieces, including Julia Jackson Duckworth, recently widowed, and her children. 'Mr. Prinsep, now an invalid, was the centre of solicitude. . . . At luncheon, Mrs. Prinsep, at the head of her table, reigned over her large family party, looking like the wife of a Venetian Doge, transplanted into the nineteenth century. . . . ' Nearby lived Mrs. Nassau Senior, in failing health, and the Inverness-shire family of Fraser Tytlers, one of whose daughters became the second Mrs. Watts. Other Anglo-Indians of the 'old curry-and-rice school' came to visit, notably the Ritchies. Tennyson came almost daily to chat with 'Uncle Thoby', now blind and somewhat deaf but still vigorous in mind, and to read aloud to him the letters from his artist son Val Prinsep, who was overseas painting the 'Proclamation of the Queen as Empress of India'.

It was a severe loss to the circle when the Camerons decided in 1875 to give up their Freshwater home and return to the East. Julia had been 'slicing up Ceylon' with her hospitality and her camera, and they needed to recoup financially. Besides Mr. Cameron was homesick for scenes of his younger days, and both parents missed their four sons who were in the civil service out there. 'The striking of the tents for the Cameron household was full of characteristic unusualness . . . rooms piled up with packing-cases, while telegrams poured in and out, and friends came in crowds to say their farewell.' Many, including Anny Thackeray, went down to Southampton to see them off. 'Two coffins preceded them on board packed with glass and china, in case coffins should be unprocurable in the East. . . . [Mr. Cameron] with his bright fixed eyes and his beard "dipt in moonlight" held in one hand his ivory staff and in the other Lady Tennyson's parting gift of a pink rose; while Mrs. Cameron "grave and valiant", vociferated her final injunctions and controlled not only innumerable packages but a cow.' At the last moment, there was a shortage of English currency, and so Mrs. Cameron tipped the army of railway porters who had transferred them to the ship with copies of her mounted photographs of Carlyle or the 'quite divine' parlourmaid Madonna Mary.

The Camerons settled in a mountain house in Kalutara, south of Colombo above the sea, bosky in the woods and surrounded with pet wild life. He was happy with his poetry, pacing outdoors on the veranda, and she with photography indoors overflowing the house. They made one more brief visit to England in the summer of 1878, 'a last visit as it proved to be, of turmoil, sickness, sorrows, marriages, and deaths'. Thoby Prinsep had died the preceding February. Anny Thackeray, now Mrs. Ritchie, and the mother of a tiny daughter, wrote in her diary: 'In the evening the nurse said to me "a strange looking lady appeared after the christening and threw a white Indian shawl over the baby." I saw the white shawl, and knew it was my dear Mrs. Cameron.' At their Ceylon home, Julia Cameron died in 1879 and Mr. Cameron, at his son Hardinge's home, a few months later. Both were buried near Colombo.

Sara Prinsep, 'whose strength lay in energy rather than endurance, could not face the grim reality [of her husband's death] and collapsed; on which . . . Mrs. Herbert Duckworth . . . came to take charge of the paralysed household. . . . The beloved younger son, Major Arthur Prinsep, also appeared from India.' Mrs. Prinsep finally took the girls to settle in Brighton, and Watts returned to London. His 'real friend was Thoby Prinsep, and it was only his chivalrous wish to help' that kept him with the Prinsep ladies for a short time.

Sara consoled herself and found 'a balm for her excitable temperament in the forms and ceremonies of her religion. The ritual of the High Church appealed to her, and she became the prop of St. Michael and All Angels, whose incumbent was the Rev. C. Beanlands. As she could do nothing by halves, she threw herself with frantic zeal in the *rôle* of helper. Her first care was the surplices of the choir and clergy. . . .' She set up a laundry in her house to have them all done there, a task which made 'a considerable drain on her income'. Her eldest son, Sir Henry Prinsep, remonstrated from India, and appointed a cousin in business to make a budget for her; she was to allow herself to send only one telegram a week, and to conserve postage she was to use postcards. But as soon as the cousin's back was turned, Sara dispatched 'telegram after telegram' to all her friends and relations, telling them of his visit, and took pains to be more extravagant than ever.

Nearby in Brighton lived Dr. and Mrs. Jackson, the latter in poor health and Dr. Jackson having retired from practice in London. They had had four children: a little boy named George Corrie, who had lived to be only two and a half years old, and three daughters, all now married: Adeline, who married Halford Vaughan; Mary, who became Mrs. Herbert Fisher; and Julia, who was first Mrs. Duckworth and then Mrs. Leslie Stephen. One gathers from many hints that Maria Pattle Jackson was the most reticent of the sisters, somewhat severe and ascetic, tender-hearted and spiritual. Though now near sixty, she was still very beautiful, for as Watts explained, 'the structure of her face was so fine that the beauty of line only increased with age'. The sculptor Thomas Woolner had also appreciated her beauty; Emily Tennyson, in a letter to Julia Cameron in 1859, tells of Woolner's making portrait medallions of herself and her family, and wishes that he would use his skill to commemorate the beauty of 'the Queens and Princesses of Pattledom. . . . Words fail Mr. Woolner, all eloquent as he is, when he speaks of the Pattle sisters, especially of the beautiful Mrs. Jackson and her three beautiful daughters.' In the physical and spiritual beauty of the youngest Jackson daughter, Julia Stephen, preserved in her aunt's photographs and her daughter Virginia Woolf's pen portrait of her as Mrs. Ramsay in *To the Lighthouse*, the charm of the Pattle sisters is best perpetuated.

As for Maria Pattle Jackson's severity, Lady Troubridge records a schoolroom scrape, when she and her sister Rachel were being educated by tutors at their grandmother Sara Prinsep's house in Brighton. They were in the giggly, mischievous stage, and had teased their bald-headed English master. 'Granny . . . took counsel with her sister, Mrs. Jackson; . . . and this lady . . . was perfectly horrified, as she was a strict martinet. "Punish them, Sara, punish them," she said; and Granny came home and took her advice.'

It is curious that Louisa Pattle Bayley does not appear during the 'fifties and 'sixties among the visitors at her sisters' homes in London and the Isle of Wight, although they evidently visited her occasionally in Brighton, Midhurst, or Tunbridge. Perhaps she was merely in more straitened circumstances financially and tied down by her large family—or embarrassed by her broken nose. There were nine Bayley children, three sons and six daughters. One of the sons died in infancy, and the other two in early manhood. Augusta Prinsep Becher, though not closely related to the Bayleys, preferred Louisa and her daughters to any of her other cousins, and has left kindly records of their picnics, their music, and their visits together. Louisa Bayley survived her husband by only one month, dying in March 1873.

The youngest Pattle sister, Sophie Dalrymple, after six years of married life in Tipperah and Calcutta, returned to England

and appears to have been with her sister Sara from 1853 until 1873 or later. She was a great favourite with Watts, gave him his nickname 'Signor', and always signed herself to him 'Sorella'. He painted a 'miniature portrait of her on panel, in a green dress full of "crinkles," a string of coral beads about her neck'. She had 'red-brown hair', her 'movements were beautiful, and the soft material she wore fell into arrangements of line full of suggestion to the artist's eye'. Sophie's looks did not keep so well as her older sisters'. Lady Troubridge remembers her from the 'Briary' days as still endowed 'with the Pattle vivacity and delightfully affectionate manners'. Her sister Sara treated her 'almost as a child. She wore large plaits of red hair, and one could see that she had been beautiful, but she seemed to us incredibly old.'

Dalrymple retired from the civil service about 1873, and the family settled at the Lodge, in North Berwick in Scotland, spending part of every year in the south of France. The Dalrymples had three children: Hew (1848–68); Walter, born in 1854, who became eighth baronet in succession to his father; and Virginia Julian, who became Lady Francis Champneys. The baronetcy of Hamilton-Dalrymple, a cadet branch of the Earls of Stair, came to John Warrender Dalrymple only a few months before his death in December 1888.

The story of Virginia Pattle has been saved until the last not only because she was the most spectacularly beautiful but because she made the most brilliant marriage, to Lord Eastnor (later the Earl of Somers), a cousin of Lady Canning. The other Pattles are almost invariably identified as the sisters of Countess Somers, and popular saying linked three of them in a trio: Mrs. Prinsep as Dash, Mrs. Cameron as Talent, and Lady Somers as Beauty.

Virginia survived seven years of Calcutta and London society without getting married; no doubt her parents' illness and death in some measure discouraged marriage. But there is a wistful suggestion that she was somewhat isolated by being almost too beautiful. Thackeray made her the subject of a paper signed 'The Proser'—'On a Good-Looking Young Lady', published in *Punch*, June 8, 1850. He calls her Erminia and says that he had known her family 'long before the young lady was born. Victorina her mother, Boa her aunt, Chinchilla her grandmother—I have been intimate with every one of these

ladies: and at the table of Sabilla, her married sister, with whom
Erminia lives, have a cover laid for me whenever I choose to
ask for it.' He goes on about an affecting scene that he had
witnessed, the first introduction of the poet Timotheus (i.e.
Henry Taylor) to this enchanting beauty, upon which Taylor
wrote a poem to her. 'When Erminia got the verses and read
them, she laid them down, and . . . began to cry a little. The
verses were full of praises of her beauty. "They all tell me that,"
she said; "nobody cares for anything but that." '

Thackeray's description of Virginia in this paper evokes her
beauty: 'Fate is beneficent to a man before whose eyes at the
parks, or churches, or theatres, or public or private assemblies
it throws Erminia. To see her face is a personal kindness for
which one ought to be thankful to Fortune. . . . When she comes
into the room, it is like a beautiful air of Mozart breaking upon
you: when she passes through a ball-room, everybody turns and
asks who is that Princess, that fairy lady? Even the women,
especially those who are the most beautiful themselves, admire
her. . . .' Yet Thackeray claims that he was not in love with
her—'there are some women too handsome, as it were, for
that'—and would no more want to marry her, or expect to,
than he would Diana, the moon-goddess.

When Virginia did marry, 'the lamentations were many'.
Watts and his friends used to say jocularly that they were deeply
grieved; 'we thought she ought not to marry any *one*'. The lucky
fellow, Lord Eastnor, is said to have fallen in love with her from
seeing her portrait on a visit to Watts's studio. He and Virginia
were married on October 2, 1850, amid rejoicing of all their
friends and relations.

Watts left many pictures of her in addition to that first
silver-point that took Eastnor's eye. His next picture of her was
'almost a profile . . . showing the deep lids drooping over the
beautiful eyes. But these studies are many, one so minute that
her sister, Mrs. Cameron, always carried it inside her watchcase.' The pictures show, as Lady Troubridge points out, that
Virginia did not rely on any artificial aids to beauty—'no curls,
no frills or furbelows, no jewels; she is as God made her, a
perfectly beautiful woman. . . .' Indeed, the dress of all the
Pattle sisters 'was not quite of the fashion of that time, but de-
signed by themselves upon simple lines; it depended upon rich

colour and ample folds for its beauty, and was very individual and expressive'.

In 1858 the Eastnors bought a London house, adjoining the Edens', and Virginia devoted herself to society there and in the south of France. Her two daughters who survived, Isabel, who married Lord Henry Somerset, and Adeline, who became Lady Tavistock and eventually Duchess of Bedford, were brought up at Eastnor Castle by governesses 'in strict seclusion . . . while their exquisite mother entranced the fashionable and artistic world of London and made romantic journeys to Italy. . . .' Lady Troubridge recalls her great-aunt, Countess Somers, when she was 'middle-aged and rather awe-inspiring', a great lady with manners that were 'a combination of stateliness and caressing kindness. . . . Her nature was far more complex than one would have thought by looking at her face. She had an immense power of loving, allied to an imperious and passionately impulsive temperament . . . [and] a strain of practical shrewdness.' After the scandal of Isabel's separation from her husband—an affair badly mismanaged by Lady Somers, who 'descended on the situation, in a whirlwind of French horror and dramatic tableau'—Virginia retired to Aix-les-Bains, and taking a house at Grésy, 'she exercised a gracious and queen-like and slightly theatrical hospitality'. She often came to see Mr. and Mrs. Watts, who spent part of their honeymoon at Aix in 1888, and 'seldom empty-handed. She brought flowers and books, or it might be a loaf of home-made bread. And we drove to see her at home in her garden of a thousand roses.'

Lady Somers and Lady Dalrymple survived into the twentieth century, the only ones of the Pattle great-aunts whom Vanessa and Virginia Stephen, in the early days of the Bloomsbury Group, could have known besides their own grandmother, Mrs. Jackson. Lady Somers died in London on September 29, 1910; and Lady Dalrymple died on June 16, 1911. Such was the last of the Pattle sisters. 'The names of those who were subjects in [their] kingdom would almost comprise the history of [their] time. . . . Whatever may be said, beauty does not pass away. The thought of it is a possession from one generation to another.'

3

Julia Prinsep Duckworth Stephen, née Jackson (1846–1895)

IN 1848, at the age of two, Julia Jackson came to England from Calcutta with her mother, Maria Pattle Jackson, and her aunts, Julia Cameron and Virginia Pattle. Charles Hay Cameron and his family were retiring permanently to England, but Dr. Jackson remained behind in Calcutta until 1855. So Mrs. Jackson, little Julia, and her two older sisters, Adeline and Mary, lived about, as visitors at their relatives' homes in or near London, or in lodgings at Brighton near Louisa Pattle Bayley, until Dr. Jackson rejoined them and they settled at Brighton.

How the little girls were educated is never mentioned, but probably by the usual Victorian method of resident governesses, often, no doubt, in combination with Bayley, Cameron, Prinsep, and other cousins. Julia is said to have been frequently at Little Holland House, as a child and young girl, where she was admired and painted by Watts and Burne-Jones, and where she became acquainted with the Thackeray girls and all the hosts of kin and their friends. Then there would be visits to the Camerons at Putney and later at Freshwater. Her Aunt Julia photographed her often; one of the best-known of these pictures appears in Maitland's *Life and Letters of Leslie Stephen* opposite page 312. It is a full-face portrait of a large-eyed, solemn, madonnaesque teenager, in a plain dark dress, with a white ruche around the high neck. Allowing for the prolonged, unblinking stare required by Aunt Julia's slow-moving shutter, one is still puzzled by this picture, and by other candid snapshots of her, to divine the powerful charm of Julia Jackson. Yet she had any number of suitors and all her life received the cordial admiration of both sexes.

Fortunately, she was endowed with lively intelligence, common sense, and courage, as well as with the strictness of character, the Victorian feminine virtues, and the sense of duty to be expected from the upbringing afforded by the Jackson parents. There was not much exaggeration in the worship given to her as if to a saint. But she had enough of the Pattle spontaneity, extravagance, and humour to save her from being sentimental or stodgy like other members of her family.

Leslie Stephen first met her when he was an occasional Sunday afternoon visitor at Little Holland House between 1864 and 1867, the year he married Minny Thackeray. Julia was one of that set of young people whom he was getting to know through the George Smiths and the Tom Hughes family. Tom Hughes's sister is said to have told him 'before he married Minny that he ought to consider Julia Jackson carefully'. Julia and Leslie, and no doubt Minny too, were among the guests at Anny Thackeray's birthday picnic on June 9, 1866, somewhere in the country near London, with 'luncheon at the Inn, tea under great trees, carts to the station, Mrs. Sartoris singing'. But Stephen, says Annan, 'dared hardly think that [Julia] would cast her eyes in his direction. When she became engaged to Herbert Duckworth, he felt "a sharp pang of jealousy," possibly because Duckworth was only a year younger than himself [i.e. thirty-three to Julia's twenty]; and hearing Duckworth described as "the perfect type of public school man" confirmed Stephen in his self-distrust and convinced him that such beautiful creatures as Julia Jackson were not for crotchety intellectuals like him.' But 'even when he married Minny', a few months after the Duckworth wedding, 'he had been keen to make a good impression on Julia'.

Herbert Duckworth, a barrister, was of a family of landed gentry in Somersetshire, who would have had Anglo-Indian connections with the Pattle sisters' families. He and Julia settled in the respectable neighbourhood of Hyde Park Gate South, across from Kensington Gardens, and proceeded to bring up a family, the third child, Gerald, however, not being born until two months after Herbert Duckworth's untimely death in the autumn of 1870. Leslie Stephen recorded in the 'Mausoleum Book' that Duckworth was not well during 1870, but his illness did not seem alarming; in September, he and Julia enjoyed a visit to the Vaughans in Pembrokeshire; some undue physical exertion ruptured an abscess, which brought on pain, and death followed within twenty-four hours, on the 19th of September,

1870. After scarcely four years of marriage, Julia was left a widow, at the age of twenty-four, with three small children to bring up alone. This shock, with her life 'all a shipwreck', as she put it to Stephen later, robbed her of whatever happiness she had expected in life and even of her religious faith. Stephen, however, admired most of all in his wife-to-be the way in which she digested her sorrow and turned it into a capacity for surpassingly sympathetic care of others in any kind of distress.

Anny and Minny Thackeray Stephen had long been beloved friends of Julia Duckworth, and they must have been drawn closer to her in her grief, though she retreated from all society for a number of years. She would, however, have been in a position to follow Leslie Stephen's advancing career in letters, and she found herself admiring his articles and sympathizing with his liberal, agnostic views. When the similar blow descended on Leslie of losing his wife Minny in 1875, they had in common their sad untimely bereavement. Leslie must have begun leaning on her sympathy, as well as on her advice in dealing with Anny and his orphaned child Laura. It is easy to see why he moved to a house neighbouring hers in Hyde Park Gate, though he did not realize until 1877 that what he felt for Julia was a passionate, adoring love much stronger than their supposed fraternal affection. He began wooing her and after a year succeeded in persuading her to marry him.

From the night of January 5, 1878, when Julia finally said 'Yes' to Leslie, until their wedding on March 26th, she was away on one of her errands of mercy, taking care of Uncle Thoby Prinsep in his last illness and of her Aunt Sara, in Freshwater and Brighton, whither Leslie pursued her as often as he could. For their honeymoon, they went to the Somers' Eastnor Castle, near Ledbury in the Malvern hills. Writing to J. R. Lowell from 'this gorgeous castle' only two days after the wedding, Stephen says, 'Our children are coming this afternoon, and we shall be in perfect quiet with them for the next three weeks.' But he had reason at this pinnacle of happiness to feel nothing but optimism, for once. He goes on, 'The snow is coming down as if we were in Siberia or Massachusetts. The Malverns look like mountains in the gloom and everything outside is dismal. It seems hard on the unlucky primroses, which were coming out in a reckless way all round us. But inside we are very cosy by huge coal-fires, and I think of a poet [i.e., of course, Lowell] who has sung the praises of fireplaces and Nicotia, and hope that we shall worship that goddess together again some day— somebody here remarks that I write very slowly. . . .' Three weeks later, in another letter to Lowell, Stephen sums it up: 'Tomorrow we go to town, and this afternoon I am in the agonies of packing up and separating my own books from those which I have borrowed from the library here—I wish it was mine! . . . I could stay here with pleasure for an indefinite time; but Hyde Park Gate South has its charms too, and I suppose that solitude, even of this variety, would be corrupting in the long run. It has already made me hate pen and ink as I think that I never hated them before. I must write a little for very substantial reasons. . . .'

Stephen, and his daughter, little eight-year-old Laura, now recognized as incurably deficient mentally, moved into Julia's house, No. 13 Hyde Park Gate South (it was later renumbered No. 22). Anny Thackeray had been married to Richmond Ritchie and was no longer part of Stephen's household. Now to the Duckworth children, George, Stella, and Gerald, Leslie and Julia added four others of their own, Vanessa, Thoby, Virginia, and Adrian. The pressure of literary work to keep up with mounting household expenses is not surprising, but it only added to Stephen's customary phobias and insecurities. From 1881 to 1891, he had the *Dictionary of National Biography* on his hands, the 'Dixery', or as Thoby called it once the 'contradictionary'. Only by extraordinary powers of concentration and application could such an enormous output of literary work be accomplished as remains to Leslie Stephen's lasting fame; he was a mountaineer of letters as well as of the Alps. But the strain on Julia of running the household and keeping him well and happy was devastating.

Nevertheless, their home was very happy for a number of years, with good friends frequenting the semi-monthly Sunday tramps that Leslie instituted in 1879, and alternatively Julia's Sunday afternoons 'at home'. By July 1880, the Lowells had arrived in London for J. R. Lowell's five-year term as 'his excellency', the American Minister. He had been a warm friend of Stephen's since 1863 and had met Julia in the summer of 1877; now he became one of her adorers. His many letters to Julia Stephen, addressing her as 'Dear Superexcellence', reflect not only Lowell's charm but an endearing picture of Julia's social character. The Stephens dined with the Lowells customarily every fortnight, and he came often to their house. Many other writers, artists, and musicians were among their visitors, besides the hosts of relatives, especially the Fisher and Vaughan nephews and nieces and their suitors. Julia, like a true Pattle, was an enthusiastic match-maker. George Meredith and Henry James were among the literary friends. The story of Henry James at the family tea-table with the Stephens, related by Leonard Woolf, in *Sowing*, p. 109, gives a character-istic picture both of James and of the Stephen family: The Stephens told Woolf that 'when they were children and Henry James came to tea, or some other meal, which he often did, he had a habit' of tilting his chair back, balancing on the two back legs, 'maintaining equilibrium by just holding on to the edge of the table', while he talked. 'As the long sentences untwined themselves, the chair would tilt slowly backwards and all the children's eyes were fixed on it, fearing and hoping that at last it would overbalance backwards and deposit Henry James on the floor. Time after time he would just recover himself, but then indeed at last it one day happened; the chair went over and the novelist was on the floor, undismayed, unhurt, and after a moment completing his sentence.'

Another tea-table story is recounted by William Rothenstein which must date from about 1890. Rothenstein had known George Duckworth in Paris and had become acquainted with the Stephen family through him and a mutual art-student friend, named Studd. Leslie Stephen filled Rothenstein with awe. 'He came down to the family tea, which was held in the basement. George was cheerful and talkative, but his sister Stella, and Virginia and Vanessa . . . in plain black dresses with white lace collars and wrist bands, looking as though they had walked straight out of a canvas by Watts or Burne-Jones, rarely spoke. Beautiful as they were, they were not more beauti-ful than their mother.' Once he 'had the temerity to ask her to sit to me for a drawing; with her gracious nature she could not say no. When the drawing was done she looked at it, then handed it in silence to her daughter. The others came up and looked over her shoulder; finally it reached Leslie Stephen. The

consternation was general. I was already looked on with
suspicion, for in those days Whistler, whose disciple I was known
to be, was anathema in Burne-Jones' and Watts' circles. The
alarm must have spread upstairs; for a message came down from
old Mrs. Jackson, Mrs. Leslie Stephen's mother, and the drawing was taken up for her to see. A confirmed invalid, Mrs.
Jackson had not come down from her room for many years;
but on seeing the drawing she rang for a stick, like the Baron
calling for his boots, and prepared to give me a piece of her
mind. I can still hear the thump of her stick as she came heavily
downstairs; and the piece of her mind which she gave me was a
solid one.'

Mrs. Jackson was now widowed, Dr. Jackson having died
at Brighton, in March 1887. Enjoying poor health as she
continued to do, she divided her time among her daughters
and at Bath and Malvern, but stayed principally with the
Stephens, until her death in February 1892. No. 22 had long
since been vastly enlarged with the addition of extra rooms and
upper storeys, so that it could accommodate the whole family,
including Laura, who remained at home until 1891, when she
had to be retired to a home in the country. From the top floors
with the nursery and Leslie's study and library, it was seven
flights down to the basement, with the kitchens presided over
by Sophy, the marvellous, devoted, and long-reigning cook,
who continued to serve the Stephen children long after both
their parents had died. 'One day,' wrote Sophy to Virginia in
1936, 'your beloved Mother found me in the kitchen shelling
peas, and said thats whot I like to see you doing wait until I
fetch Miss Stella to take a snap of you.' Quentin Bell 'deduces'
from the newspaper produced by Virginia and Vanessa, 1891–
92, the 'Hyde Park Gate News', a convincing picture of the
household: 'In addition to the eight children there were seven
servants', including principally Sophy. 'Dogs play an important
part in their lives and seem to have been more ferocious then
than now; there are also rats, bugs and relations. . . . The usual
joys and calamities of family life are recorded: lamps flare,
pipes burst, children fall ill, brothers go off to school, there are
visits to the circus and the zoo; but the grand event of the year
is the summer exodus to Cornwall.'

Indeed, Julia would not have had time for many excursions

away from this demanding household, unless she took it with
her. She did once or twice go to Switzerland with Leslie, and she
would visit her sisters and other relatives briefly. But the principal relief from the London demands was afforded by the
annual three-months sojourn somewhere in Cornwall, from
1882 to 1894 always at Talland House, St. Ives, the lease of
which Leslie Stephen purchased in 1881. His description of the
place in a letter to Mrs. W. K. Clifford, dated July 25, 1884,
evokes its pleasures: 'We are here on a lovely blowing breezy
day: the air is delicious—pure Atlantic breezes . . . and it is as
soft as silk; it has a fresh sweet taste like new milk; and it is so
clear that we see thirty miles of coast as plainly as we see the
back of Queen's Gate from our drawing-room window in
London. We have a little garden [of only two acres], which is
not much to boast of; and yet it is a dozen little gardens each
full of romance for the children—lawns surrounded by flowering
hedges, and intricate thickets of gooseberries and currants, and
remote nooks of potatoes and peas, and high banks, down
which you can slide in a sitting posture, and corners in which
you come upon unexpected puppies—altogether a pocket-
paradise with a sheltered cove of sand in easy reach (for 'Ginia
even) just below. Also there is a railway station between us and
the said cove. . . . It *is* rather solitary and far off. . . .'
    The railway station was the end of the branch line to St. Ives
from the station at St. Erth's, where visitors could board or
disembark on the main line; Lowell tended to identify Julia as
St. Erth, claiming that though he preferred Whitby to Cornwall, yet 'Cornwall has St. Erth's in it, where sometimes one
has beatific visions.' He and all the other familiars of their
London hospitality and many more besides would come to
stay with the Stephens for a week or more at a time, enjoying
the 'casual' and 'untidy' life. Long walks, botanizing and 'bug
hunting', games of cricket on the lawn, and the pleasures of
the sea absorbed them all. William Fisher ('The Admiral')
'remembered his aunt Julia bobbing about in the water in a
large black hat'. Julia also maintained her missions of benevolence and nursing among the poor folk of St. Ives; in later years
a Nursing Fund was established there in her memory, and her
name was remembered 'with affection and fervent gratitude'.
    Disasters began to overtake the Stephen family in the late

1880's, sicknesses and deaths, of friends and family members. Leslie Stephen himself had more than one breakdown between 1889 and 1891, when Julia and George Smith prevailed upon him to give up the editorship of the *Dictionary*. Every sad event made increasingly heavy burdens for Julia. Everyone laid demands upon her. 'After her death,' Bell records, 'Virginia found in her mother's travelling desk all the letters received one morning at Talland House and brought to London to be answered. There was a letter from a woman whose daughter had been betrayed, a letter from her son George, one from her sister Mary Fisher, one from a nurse who was out of work; there were begging letters, there were many pages from a girl who had quarrelled with her parents. Everyone demanded some kind of help or sympathy, everyone knew that, from her, they would get it. . . . And so she exhausted herself. Still young in years, she had raced through a lifetime in altruistic work and at length her physical resistance burnt out.' After an attack of influenza she went into a swift decline and died on May 5, 1895.

This account of Julia Stephen's life has been pieced together thus far from a selection of facts contained in biographies. But to know the woman herself, we have also the testimony in the descriptions of her composed by Leslie Stephen; one is the passage from 'Forgotten Benefactors', cited in part above, which is a kind of sermonette on the text 'She was a phantom of delight', and the other is the substance of the 'Mausoleum Book', which Stephen wrote directly after Julia's death for the private edification of his children, but from which some quotations have been published by various writers. These descriptions, however, are probably not altogether objective, since the first is coloured by Stephen's purpose in his address to the Ethical Society, and both are the expression of his idol-worship of Julia and his self-abasement in comparison to her. Probably the best of the 'Mausoleum Book' impression of her is phrased by Noel Annan, who apparently selected and rewrote portions of it, reading between Stephen's lines, and presenting Julia's personality, as Stephen did, in favourable contrast to her husband's.

Stephen 'worshipped Julia, desired to transform her into an apotheosis of motherhood, but treated her in the home as someone who should be at his beck and call, support him in every emotional crisis, order the minutiae of his life and then submit to his criticism in those household matters of which she was mistress. If a child was late for dinner, it must have been maimed or killed in an accident; and that would be her fault. He would sulk if things did not go his way; if it was suggested that he take a hot bath on coming in soaked with rain from a walk, he would consider his manliness impugned and then like a child pout with injured pride and refuse a piece of his favourite cake at tea. Stephen had cause for guilt. His wife was more remarkable than he. Julia Stephen's memorial was carved by her daughter in the characters of Mrs. Ambrose, Mrs. Hilbery and Mrs. Ramsay; and this is fitting, for Virginia Woolf inherited from her mother much of her sensibility and even an echo of her style. Julia's single publication is lost in oblivion yet it reveals her character as surely as Virginia Woolf's portraits. It is about nursing and called *Notes for Sick Rooms*. Imaginative in that it brings to mind all the details unobserved by the sage, it combines an exquisite sensibility towards other people's sufferings with exceedingly practical advice on how to alleviate them. "The origin of most things," she begins, "has been decided on, but the origin of crumbs in bed has never excited sufficient attention among the scientific world"—and from there she analyses the almost impossible task of getting rid of them. . . . She responded to other people's feelings instinctively; she could heal a child's wound before it was given and read thoughts before they were uttered, and her sympathy was like the touch of a butterfly, delicate and remote—for she knew what it was to live an inner life and respected other people's privacy. Leslie thought himself a friend in need, but she knew how to translate sympathy into action. Leslie ploughed furrows of ratiocination to reach conclusions, she had intuitively reached them and acted upon them before he arrived.'

Quentin Bell agrees with Noel Annan that Virginia Woolf's portrait of her mother as Mrs. Ramsay is more truthful than her father's. Annan calls *To the Lighthouse* 'the fiction of fact'. It is nevertheless fiction, which, it seems to me, stresses the Pattle side of Julia's character perhaps more than objective fact would justify. However, it may be useful to consider Virginia Woolf's artful portrayal in the light shed by Pattledom.

She obviously intended to call attention to her mother's Pattle background, as well as to produce a truly autobiographical and biographical memoir in *To the Lighthouse*. In *A Writer's Diary* (p. 75), we read that she first planned it thus: 'to have father's character done complete in it; and mother's; and St. Ives; and childhood; and all the usual things I try to put in—life, death, etc.' At this point, in the summer of 1925, she thought her father's character would be the centre of the book, 'sitting in a boat reciting We perished, each alone, while he crushes a dying mackerel'. But in fact, the novel's centre turns out to be her mother's character. The whole life of the Ramsay family and of their visitors at their summer home in the Hebrides (transmuted from St. Ives) centres in Mrs. Ramsay; living or dead, she obsesses the attention of the other characters and of the reader; she is the commanding presence in the work. Later in the *Diary* (p. 106) Mrs. Woolf records how Vanessa reacted to the novel when it had been published: 'Nessa enthusiastic—a sublime, almost upsetting spectacle. She says it is an amazing portrait of mother; a supreme portrait painter; has lived in it; found the rising of the dead almost painful.'

In considering the character of Mrs. Ramsay in the oblique light thrown on her (and back of her on Julia Stephen) from some of the allegedly non-fictional material about her maternal ancestors, the Pattle women, we must recognize that it can only be an oblique light, because it clashes with the colour and tone of Virginia Woolf's novel. *To the Lighthouse* is invested with an amber glow of nostalgia, a beautiful atmosphere, serious for all its humour, and full of pathos; whereas it must be confessed that the aura of the Pattle sisters tends to be farcical and boisterous. Early in the novel we read that Mrs. Ramsay 'had . . . in her veins the blood of that very noble, if slightly mythical, Italian house, whose daughters, scattered about English drawing-rooms in the nineteenth century, had lisped so charmingly, had stormed so wildly, and all her wit and bearing and her temper came from them, and not from the sluggish English, or the cold Scotch. . . .' (P. 17.) For 'Italian house' we should read French, i.e. the l'Etangs, for 'sluggish English' the Pattles, and the 'cold Scotch' would be derived from Dr. John Jackson, poor man, who for all his worth in medicine has never been referred to as anything but a 'nonentity' in family or social life.

The element of physical beauty was the passport of the Pattle

sisters to fame and to Victorian drawing-rooms, frequented by
artists, poets, and statesmen, all lovers of the beautiful. The
Pattle women were born to it; it was a family inheritance as
conditioning as wealth or social station. One and all, they seem
to have been slightly bored, even distressed, by their own beauty
and the pother it made, the effect of it on their men friends. This
is true, apparently, of Virginia Woolf as well as of her mother.
To quote from *To the Lighthouse*, here is young Mr. Tansley
reacting to it in Mrs. Ramsay: '. . . all at once he realised that it
was this: . . . she was the most beautiful person he had ever seen.
With stars in her eyes and veils in her hair, with cyclamen and
wild violets—what nonsense was he thinking? She was fifty at
least; she had eight children.' (P. 25.) And here is Mr. Bankes,
with a more sophisticated appreciation: 'But was it nothing
but looks, people said? What was there behind it—her beauty
and splendour? Had he blown his brains out, they asked, had
he died the week before they were married . . . Or was there
nothing? nothing but an incomparable beauty which she
lived behind, and could do nothing to disturb? . . . "Nature
has but little clay," said Mr. Bankes once, much moved by her
voice on the telephone, though she was only telling him a fact
about a train, "like that of which she moulded you." He saw
her at the end of the line very clearly Greek, straight, blue-eyed.
How incongruous it seemed to be telephoning to a woman like
that. . . . "Yet she's no more aware of her beauty than a child,"
. . . for always, he thought, there was something incongruous
to be worked into the harmony of her face. She clapped a
deer-stalker's hat on her head; she ran across the lawn in
galoshes to snatch a child from mischief . . . as if her beauty
bored her and all that men say of beauty, and she wanted only
to be like other people, insignificant.' (Pp. 46–8.)

But the Pattle ladies would not have become the legend they
did if they had been nothing but beautiful, striking to look at.
They also brimmed over with personality and energy and were
on the whole full of solid Victorian virtues and good works. So
too with Mrs. Ramsay; with the socks, tobacco, old magazines
for the lighthouse keepers, and her concern for the poor—
sometimes with the social worker's approach: 'she ruminated
the . . . problem, of rich and poor, and the things she saw with
her own eyes, weekly, daily, here or in London, when she visited

this widow, or that struggling wife in person with a bag on her arm and a note-book and pencil with which she wrote down in columns carefully ruled for the purpose wages and spendings, employment and unemployment, in the hope that thus she would cease to be a private woman whose charity was half a sop to her own indignation, half a relief to her own curiosity, and become what with her untrained mind she greatly admired, an investigator, elucidating the social problem.' (Pp. 17–18.) Here we see reflected clearly the Julia Stephen who wrote *Notes for Sick Rooms*. It was, indeed, a Pattle family attitude to take an interest in the sufferings of the poor, as we have seen in some of the actions of Sara Prinsep and Julia Cameron, the most ebullient of the sisters in their generation.

Mrs. Ramsay, in the novel, tries to pass on to her daughters her own concern and sympathy for lonely lighthouse keepers and all the other sufferers of this world, including poor young Mr. Tansley, whom the children were inclined openly to scorn: ' "Nonsense!" She turned with severity upon Nancy. He had not chased them, she said. He had been asked. . . . She was now formidable to behold, and it was only in silence, looking up from their plates, after she had spoken so severely about Charles Tansley, that her daughters, Prue, Nancy, Rose—could sport with infidel ideas which they had brewed for themselves of a life different from hers; in Paris, perhaps; a wilder life; not always taking care of some man or other; for there was in all their minds a mute questioning of deference and chivalry, of the Bank of England and the Indian Empire, of ringed fingers and lace, though to them all there was something in this of the essence of beauty, which called out the manliness in their girlish hearts, and made them, as they sat at table beneath their mother's eye, honour her strange severity, her extreme courtesy, like a Queen's raising from the mud to wash a beggar's dirty foot. . . .' (Pp. 13–14.)

In fact Mrs. Ramsay's old-world courtliness, her reverence for the masculine sex and her protective attitude towards men, giving way in most matters, triumphing in others, and her inveterate match-making and valuing of marriage and mother-hood are as much marks of her Victorian Pattle family inheri-tance as her good works. Closer to Julia Stephen's identity is the occasional questioning that Mrs. Ramsay allows herself

towards the worth of these Victorian attitudes, and her private
repudiation of conventional religion, when she swiftly condemns
herself for uttering the pious Victorian tag, 'We are all in the
hands of the Lord', in which she does not herself believe.

The Pattle women's and Mrs. Ramsay's devotion to matrimony and the importance of women as wives and mothers seems
almost more French than British. Lily Briscoe puzzles over it,
as she endeavours to capture in her painting the very spirit
of Mrs. Ramsay; it was something more than beauty and
goodness: 'What was the spirit in her, the essential thing, by
which, had you found a crumpled glove in the corner of a sofa,
you would have known it, from its twisted finger, hers indis-
putably? She was like a bird for speed, an arrow for directness.
She was wilful; she was commanding. . . . She opened bedroom
windows. She shut doors. . . . Arriving late at night, with a
light tap on one's bedroom door, wrapped in an old fur coat
(for the setting of her beauty was always that—hasty, but apt),
she would enact again whatever it might be—Charles Tansley
losing his umbrella; Mr. Carmichael snuffling and sniffing; Mr.
Bankes saying, "The vegetable salts are lost." All this she would
adroitly shape; even maliciously twist; and, moving over to the
window, in pretence that she must go,—it was dawn, she could
see the sun rising,—half turn back, more intimately, but still
always laughing, insist that she must, Minta must, they all must
marry, since in the whole world whatever laurels might be
tossed to her . . . or triumphs won by her . . . an unmarried
woman has missed the best of life. The house seemed full of
children sleeping and Mrs. Ramsay listening; shaded lights
and regular breathing.' (Pp. 76–7.)

Mrs. Ramsay's matchmaking of Paul and Minta and her ideas
for matching Lily and Mr. Bankes are reflections of the same
sort of activity in the operations of her salon-leader aunt, Sara
Prinsep, as in the case of Watts and Ellen Terry. Julia Stephen
herself advised Watts not to dally in his resolution to marry
Mary Fraser Tytler as his second wife: 'if you don't take care I
will make Leslie put on his cassock again and marry you off
hand. . . .' But to some, this affectionate interference appeared
merely bossiness and meddling. Mrs. Ramsay herself is aware of
this unfavourable view: 'she was driven on, too quickly she
knew, almost as if it were an escape for her too, to say that

people must marry; people must have children. Was she wrong in this, she asked herself . . . wondering if she had indeed put any pressure upon Minta, who was only twenty-four, to make up her mind. She was uneasy. . . . Was she not forgetting again how strongly she influenced people?' (Pp. 92–3.) A woman 'had once accused her of "robbing her of her daughter's affections"; something [Minta Doyle's mother] had said made her remember that charge again. Wishing to dominate, wishing to interfere, making people do what she wished—that was the charge against her, and she thought it most unjust.' (P. 88.) The Pattle sisters, particularly Julia Cameron, often felt that their boundless, sometimes gratuitous, benevolences—like their beauty—were not rightly understood. Aunt Julia Cameron, however, represents the roughest side of the Pattle women's overflowing vitality, a farcical version of the managing matriarch, as opposed to Mrs. Ramsay's gentler imperiousness. More like the rest of her Pattle relations are Mrs. Ramsay's hospitality (always asking 'too many people to stay' and having to 'lodge some in the town'—p. 13) and her skill as a hostess at the dinner table, her ideas about cooking and housekeeping, her feminine helplessness with money matters, and above all her mercurial temperament. In these traits, she is pure Pattle.

Surely the prolonged scene of the large family dinner party in *To the Lighthouse* is a perfect exemplification of this characteristic Pattle talent—the art of the hostess. Life even in a summer house in the Hebrides is to be savoured with ceremony and graciousness, with jewels, and a beautiful centrepiece of fruit and shells, with candles, and the Boeuf en Daube—' "it is a French recipe of my grandmother's," said Mrs. Ramsay, speaking with a ring of pleasure in her voice. Of course it was French. What passes for cookery in England is an abomination (they agreed). It is putting cabbages in water. It is roasting meat till it is like leather. It is cutting off the delicious skins of vegetables. "In which," said Mr. Bankes, "all the virtue of the vegetable is contained." And the waste, said Mrs. Ramsay. A whole French family could live on what an English cook throws away.' (Pp. 151–2.) So Mrs. Ramsay, making small talk, exerting her social skill to draw out the company, weaves the spell of the feast that is true society. 'It partook, she felt, carefully helping Mr. Bankes to a specially tender piece, of

eternity. . . . "Yes," she assured William Bankes, "there is plenty
for everybody." "Andrew," she said, "hold your plate lower, or
I shall spill it." (The Boeuf en Daube was a perfect triumph.)
Here, she felt, putting the spoon down, was the still space that
lies about the heart of things, where one could move or rest . . .'
while her company, now thoroughly stimulated, talk easily of
Voltaire and Madame de Staël, 'on the character of Napoleon;
on the French system of land tenure; on Lord Rosebery; on
Creevey's Memoirs: she let it uphold her and sustain her, this
admirable fabric of the masculine intelligence, which ran up
and down, crossed this way and that, like iron girders spanning
the swaying fabric, upholding the world. . . .' (Pp. 158–9.) At
last the whole woven edifice of nourishment, beauty, love, and
intelligence rises to a climax in the reciting of poetry. As Mrs.
Ramsay leaves the dining-room, happy that even the reluctant
Augustus Carmichael 'has bowed to her as if he did her homage',
she hesitates at the threshold to look back on the scene even
now changing. 'It had become, she knew, giving one last look
at it over her shoulder, already the past.' (P. 168.)

One consideration remains, about Virginia Woolf's extraordinary success in characterizing her mother as Mrs. Ramsay,
and that is an item to marvel over: Virginia was only thirteen
years old when her mother, Mrs. Stephen, died, and the period
recreated in the first part of *To the Lighthouse* represents still
earlier years, when Virginia, like Cam, was perhaps only eight.
Is it possible that a mind that young, even the mind of a genius,
could absorb so many impressions, could understand so profoundly? Of course there were repeated and later visits to St.
Ives, and of course she could remember certain things that
touched herself closely—like the skull of the animal nailed on
her bedroom wall—symbol of terror and death that her mother
winds out of the child's sight with her shawl, 'round and round
and round', and then turns into an object of beauty and
imagination. (Pp. 171–2.) The truth must be that Mrs. Woolf
created Mrs. Ramsay out of levels of her own consciousness and
memories buried very deep, as well as from known biographical
facts and family legends; out of the fact that she was her
mother's own daughter and able to achieve a kind of unity with
her that Lily Briscoe (mask for Virginia Woolf the novelist)
desires, but despairs of reaching with the conscious mind.

Mrs. Woolf has Mrs. Ramsay think of that involvement, prophetically, though with human blindness attaching it to the wrong people—to Paul and Minta, instead of to her daughters, the artists-to-be. 'They would, she thought, going on again, however long they lived, come back to this night; this moon; this wind; this house: and to her too. It flattered her, where she was most susceptible of flattery, to think how, wound about in their hearts, however long they lived she would be woven; and this, and this, and this, she thought, going upstairs, laughing, but affectionately, at the sofa on the landing (her mother's); at the rocking-chair (her father's) . . . it was all one stream, and chairs, tables, maps, were hers, were theirs, it did not matter whose. . . .' (Pp. 170–1.)

Mrs. Woolf's fictional creation of Mrs. Ramsay is a reflection in the world of her imagination shadowing forth the actual woman, Julia Jackson Stephen, with all her affiliations in the generations of Pattle women, and at the same time it is a universally appealing picture of womanhood. Henry James, in a touching letter of sympathy to Leslie Stephen on his loss of Julia, wrote: 'She leaves no image but that of the high enjoyment of affections and devotions—the beauty and the good she wrought and the tenderness that came back to her. Unquenchable seems to me such a presence.'

4

Jane Maria Strachey, née Grant
(1840–1928)

VIRGINIA WOOLF began her diary for 1919 by looking forward to the day when she would write her memoirs, perhaps when she was fifty, not old, but sufficiently elderly. Recognizing that her journals would provide the basis, she then and there reviewed her current circle of friends, beginning with the MacCarthys and going next to the Stracheys. Most of the latter she lumped together as all very worthy people—loyal, honest, rational, intellectually spiritual—but prosaic and shorn of atmosphere. Lytton and his mother, however, she would except always; Lytton she obviously admired very much, and Lady Strachey, she implies, was an extraordinary person. When in January 1928 Mrs. Woolf records that Lady Strachey is slowly fading away, her grief is evident. In December, after attending the majestic old lady's funeral, she remarks that she could not feel any emotion at it, becuase she had already suffered in imagination the grief of her loss.

Mrs. Woolf's memorial tribute to Lady Strachey, published in the *Nation and the Athenaeum*, Dec. 22, 1928, reveals the reasons for her admiration and love: Lady Strachey was 'the type of the Victorian woman at her finest—many-sided, vigorous, adventurous, advanced. . . . With her large and powerful frame, her strongly marked features, her manner that was so cordial, so humorous, and yet perhaps a little formidable, she seemed cast on a larger scale, made of more massive material than the women of to-day. . . . One could easily imagine how, had she been a man, she would have ruled a province or administered a Government department. . . . But in addition . . . she was emphatically a mother and a wife. Even while she wrote dispatches at her husband's dictation and debated—for she was in the counsels of the men who governed India— . . . she was bringing up, now in India, now in England, a family of ten children.'

In the 'vast Victorian household' at Lancaster Gate, where Virginia Woolf had first known her, Lady Strachey presided, 'herself a little absent-minded, a little erratic, but nevertheless the controller and inspirer of it all, now wandering through the rooms with a book, now teaching a group of young people the steps of a Highland reel, now plunging into ardent debate about politics or literature, now working out, with equal intentness, some puzzle in a penny paper which if solved would provide her with thirty shillings a week and a workman's cottage for life. . . .

'She was an omnivorous reader. She had her hands upon the whole body of English literature, from Shakespeare to Tennyson, with the large loose grasp that was so characteristic of the cultivated Victorian.' Mrs. Woolf goes on to tell of her reading aloud, 'one of her great natural gifts', and 'when the reading was over, she would launch out into stories of the past . . . of Pattles and Prinseps; of bygone beauties and scandals—for though she observed the conventions she was not in the least a prude; of Indian society fifty years, eighty years, a hundred years ago. For she had the Scottish love of following family histories and tracing the friendships and alliances of the present back to their roots in the past. Thus a haphazard party would come in her presence to have a patriarchal air, as she recalled the memories and the marriages that had bound parents and grandparents together years ago, in the distant past.'

In a word, Lady Strachey epitomized for her children and their friends the Victorian and the Anglo-Indian family pasts that they shared; while they were in rebellion against all that, and wanted to change features of their heritage that they deplored, they could not help being influenced by such a dominant character. Chief among these influences were her political liberalism, especially her feminism, and her enthusiastic love of literature, conveyed often through expert reading aloud.

Allowing for Mrs. Woolf's natural overflow of sentiment in the tribute quoted above, her portrait sketch is nevertheless realistic. It is borne out by the other pictures of Lady Strachey now available in print, some in words, and some in paint or photography. Charles Richard Sanders first gathered together facts and anecdotes about her and published them, with two photographs of her, in *The Strachey Family, 1588–1932* (Duke

University Press, 1953). Michael Holroyd, adding another
photograph, brings Lady Strachey more vividly to life in his
two-volume biography of Lytton Strachey (Heinemann, 1967–
1968), though of course she remains in the background of that
work and—after the introductory pages on her—is seen from
Lytton's perspective, sometimes rather ambiguously. The best
impression of her in writing is to be found in Betty Askwith's
brilliant evocation of the Richard Strachey family during 1884–
1907, in their Lancaster Gate house in London (*Two Victorian
Families*, Chatto & Windus, 1971), which includes a much more
appealing snapshot of Lady Strachey leaning on her bicycle,
taken perhaps about 1897, when she was still '*the* Mrs. Richard
Strachey'. The most revealing visual image now published is
doubtless the reproduction of Carrington's portrait of her (in
Carrington: Letters and Extracts from her Diaries, ed. David Garnett,
Jonathan Cape, 1970). Carrington, with her artist's vision,
really saw the essential woman. She describes the experience in
her letter to Lytton of November 24, 1920: 'This morning I went
at eleven o'ck to paint Her Ladyship. She is superb. It's rather
stupid to tell *you* this. But I was completely overcome by her
grandeur, and wit. I am painting her against the bookcase
sitting full length in a chair, in a wonderful robe which goes into
great El Greco folds. It is lined with orange. So the effect is a
very sombre picture with a black dress, and mottled cloak, and
then brilliant orange edges down the front of her dress. She
looks like the Queen of China, or one of El Greco's Inquisitors.'
(P. 170.)

One might hark back from that judgment of Lady Strachey
at eighty years of age to her own amused recollection, written
that same year, of herself, Janie Grant, aged twelve, galloping
on her pony in the country near Penang, flourishing her long
whip and imagining herself as 'Zenobia, Queen of Palmyra', a
popular novel she was then enjoying.

Jane was born at sea, on March 13, 1840, aboard the India-
man *The Earl of Hardwicke*, as she rounded the Cape of Good
Hope 'in the midst of a violent storm', en route from Bengal to
London. Her mother, going home 'on account of her health,'
was accompanied by the Grants' family doctor and his wife,
and by her three young children, John Peter III, Trevor, and
Elinor. Jane was named for her father's mother, Jane Ironside

Lady Grant of Rothiemurchus, and Maria (a good 'leg-of-mutton' name) after a favourite governess, though Mrs. Grant had been tempted to make it Undine. When the ship reached London, Jane was christened and registered as a native of Stepney, one of three parishes at that time open to choose from for British subjects born at sea.

Until Mr. Grant's furlough began in 1841, the family lived in a boarding house in London, but after his arrival they all went to Rothiemurchus in Inverness-shire, to his father's house, the Doune; Jane's first memories were of that home. She was barely four years old when her father, having to return to India, took them all by post-chaise up to London. He and Mrs. Grant and the baby Henrietta, born in 1843, set sail, leaving the four older children at a school in Highgate. This was run by a couple named Keickhoffer (he was of German origin), and of course known as 'Kickover'. 'I was not at all unhappy at school,' so Jane recalled; 'I was much the youngest there, and was petted a good deal by the older girls. I learnt to read very soon, and, as I never afterwards had my nose out of a book, I acquired the nickname "the bookworm."' The close bonds between Jane and her older sister Elinor dated from these schooldays.

For holidays, the Grant children were taken in by their relatives, usually by the George Freres in Bedford Square. Mrs. Frere was the only sister of Sir J. P. Grant I, their Rothiemurchus grandfather. Sometimes they were invited by their mother's cousin, Amelia Erskine Martin, and her family of children, also from Calcutta and nearer the Grants in age than the grown-up Frere daughters and son. And sometimes they went to their aunt in Edinburgh, Jane Grant Gibson-Craig, one of their father's two sisters. It was there that Trevor, aged ten, got into mischief by imbibing whisky during a parade in some neighbouring village. Uncle James Gibson-Craig reprimanded him: 'Ye have begun airlier than I did, me lad.' And there also, Janie lost her 'abundant fair hair', which Nellie, the old servant, who had to brush and arrange it, found a nuisance, and so clipped it all off close to the child's head, when she was preparing her one evening for the regular visit with the family downstairs.

When the boys were old enough to go to prep school, Elinor and Jane went over to Ireland to spend a year with their aunt

Mrs. Eliza Grant Smith, the other sister of J. P. Grant II, at her
estate, Baltiboys, on the river Liffey in County Wicklow. So,
before she was seven years old, Janie became acquainted with her
famous aunt whose memoirs she would edit and publish some
fifty years later. Lessons continued under the supervision of Miss
John Clerk, the governess, who accompanied the little girls back
to London in the spring; their mother had returned from India,
to remain for four years until her health was re-established.
Miss Clerk, Jane remembered, was far from well qualified as a
teacher, and she found the dreary drilling in writing, arithmetic,
French, and music very dull fare. Besides, Jane was still suffering
from the blinding headaches which had plagued her at the
Highgate school and were then attributed to a steady school diet
of roast mutton and milk pudding. But it is hard not to suppose
that they may have been a symptom of eye-strain in one who
was a bookworm and read, for example, a complete edition of
Sir Walter Scott's novels in five volumes of double-column
print.

Mrs. Grant, Miss Clerk, and the little girls, including now
their retarded sister Henrietta, and the little brother George,
lived for two years in the Paddington environment, apparently
in lodgings, and then moved in 1850 to the Marylebone section
to be next door to the Charles Plowdens. He was an uncle of
Mrs. Grant, whose maiden name was Henrietta Chichele-
Plowden. Other Plowden relatives were available, too: Walter
Plowden, newly appointed the British consul in Abyssinia, Mrs.
Grant's youngest brother, was in London for a few months in
1848; he was the one who was tragically murdered in the desert
in 1860, and then bloodily avenged by his friend, the Abys-
sinian Emperor. From another uncle, Trevor Plowden, Jane first
learned what reading aloud could mean. She had been enjoying
Washington Irving's *Life of Oliver Goldsmith* and had proceeded
to Goldsmith's poetry. Her uncle read aloud to her 'The Haunch
of Venison', entrancing her with its epistolary irony and its
opportunities for Scottish and Irish brogues.

Mrs. Grant's mother, widowed and remarried to Henry
Meredith Parker, came home from India and visited them,
but she died that same year of 1848. She was the most musical
of the Plowdens, and Grandpapa Parker loved music, too; in
his home Elinor and Jane first heard the famous violoncellist

Piatti, who became their lifelong friend. There were also dancing lessons for Elinor and Jane, from M. Delplanque, a fashionable dancing master whose father had held forth at the court of Louis XVI. The boys, John and Trevor, would occasionally be at home with them in school holidays; Janie and Trevor began to be the chums that they ever after remained. Besides, there was the Rowe family, living in the Kensington neighbourhood, whose children had been their schoolmates at Highgate, and who were treated like cousins, though they were not kin. He was a wholesale merchant, of a Devonshire family, descended, they believed, from Nicholas Rowe, the playwright. The connection with the Rowe family had begun when Mrs. Grant found a situation with Mrs. Rowe for the wet-nurse who had taken care of the baby Janie in 1841. 'Without ... the Rowes, our lives as children would have lost almost all joy and sunshine,' Lady Strachey recalled, 'to say nothing of our after family connection through the marriage of Marion Rowe to my eldest brother, and of Adeline to Cousin Bartle Frere.'

But with all these bright spots in their lives, the years in London were not ones that Jane remembered with joy; she had felt imprisoned in the school-room; and hoop-rolling in the park, her favourite outdoor amusement, was after all not very exciting. So when Mrs. Grant, now completely recovered, decided in 1851 to do the unusual thing and take the girls back with her to India, so that their father might be acquainted with them before they were grown up, Jane's life suddenly became filled with boundless delight.

They sailed from London in August on the East India Company's ship *The Trafalgar*, whose captain, Divie Robertson (pronounced 'Divvie'), was a relative by marriage of Mrs. Grant. Besides Henrietta, Janie, and Elinor, Mrs. Grant took with them her two nieces Amelia and Kate Batten, and Miss Clerk, the governess. This bevy of females had several cabins in the stern of the ship, one fitted out as their sitting-room, complete with a cottage piano, and books, and their own stock of wine, for the five-month voyage around Africa, up to Aden, and across to Calcutta.

A sea voyage, even a short one, forms an island in anyone's experience that can produce heightened sensibility and awareness. For Jane, an active girl of eleven, tall for her age, with high spirits and an outgoing, daring nature, this voyage was a great adventure. (No wonder she manoeuvred many years later to secure the same experience for her eleven-year-old son Lytton, and rejoiced in his eye-opening adventures.) There was much to observe and watch—'storms, calms, water-spouts on the horizon, flying fish, albatrosses'. The sailors fished for sharks off the stern, outside their sitting-room windows. The girls lay in their bunks at night watching the cockroaches parade across the deck above them. An eighteen-year-old Army cadet, going to join his regiment in Aden, walked the deck with Janie and read aloud to her Scott's and Byron's poetry, when she was blinded by a headache. Elinor and Jane played duets for Captain Divie in his cabin every evening—Beethoven's Symphonies and Airs out of Operas. Janie became a great favourite of the captain—she was the one who managed to persuade him not to have the midshipmen discharged, after they had got drunk on the left-over wine, which Mrs. Grant donated to their mess at the end of the voyage.

No doubt Mr. Grant came down the Hooghli River with the pilot's boat to meet them in January 1852, and escort them 'home'. He had not seen Elinor and Jane since they were very small children. For the first time, also, Jane was seeing the Indian landmarks of her family's life; they would have passed her grandfather Grant's former home on the east bank of the river fourteen miles downstream from Calcutta, near the Governor-General's summer home with its surrounding park and the zoo—one went for elephant rides in the park—and then Barrackpore, where the soldiers lived, and the crowded suburb of Serampore across the river, with its churches, temples, bazaar, ghats, and college, and a tall tree, visible for over four miles.

Home was No. 8 Elysium Row, a house near the seat of government in Calcutta. Mr. Grant was very busy in his important post of Secretary to the Government of Bengal, but there were nearly always guests at dinner, and Elinor and Jane were allowed to join the company at dessert and listen to the entertaining conversations. 'My father treated my sister and me as rational beings; allowed us to say what was in our minds; if we were wrong, showed us why; if we were right, agreed at once. I remember going in once to the evening dinner when a lively discussion was going on, and as I came in at the door,

my father called out: "We will ask Janie. Janie, which do you
think the better, 'The Traveller' or 'The Deserted Village'?"
"I like 'The Traveller,'" said I—applause from my father—
"but I *love* 'The Deserted Village'"—applause from the rest of
the company!'

Miss Clerk disappears from Lady Strachey's Memoirs at
this time, perhaps mercifully removed from the family by
matrimony, which was the usual fate of any young woman
imported from England. The girls' education proceeded infor-
mally in the family. With her father, Jane read Macaulay's
History of England, and with her mother the novels of Jane
Austen. French literature was also a topic of discussion after
supper, conducted in French, until the girls, whose knowledge
of the language had been merely drill in grammar, were
able to speak it. There were musical evenings; Mr. Grant
played the 'cello well, and liked to hold little chamber music
sessions.

Among the family's 'most intimate friends in Calcutta' were
John Dalrymple (afterwards Sir John), husband of one of
the Pattle sisters, and the William Ritchies. The Ritchie
children, 'of whom there were then only four, Pinkie and Willie
(infants in the nursery), and Gussie and Blanche, who, though
several years younger than we, were charming little companions', remained lifelong friends of Elinor and Jane. Gussie
grew up to marry 'Mr. Douglas Freshfield, the great mountain
climber, and Blanche, Mr. Warre-Cornish. Willie married
Madeleine Brookfield, and one of the later sons, Richmond,
married Annie Thackeray.' Dr. Jackson, married to Maria
Pattle, was the family physician; Jane was very fond of him
and later always rejoiced to think that her children's friends,
the Leslie Stephen children, were his grandchildren.

The two years of life in Calcutta, supplemented by the
exciting two-months visit to Penang across the Bay of Bengal,
were over all too soon, and Elinor, Henrietta, and Jane had
to go home to England to school again. In January 1854,
they set out, chaperoned by other good family friends, Sir
John and Lady Lowis; this time they went by the newly established overland route; the Suez Canal was only partly finished,
and so there was also a trek across the desert to the Mediter-
ranean; but the whole journey was thus shortened to a matter

of weeks. In England, Uncle Trevor Plowden took charge and
sent the Grant girls to join his own children at the Vicarage
School at Newbald in Yorkshire. The school was one for boys,
in a separate building adjoining the vicarage, but Nina Plowden
and her Grant cousins lived together with the vicar Mr.
Blyth's family, having their lessons in the schoolroom there,
'under the care of a good-tempered young governess, who, in
accordance with the custom of the time, gave us plenty of
lessons without teaching us anything'. Within a year, Elinor,
who had turned sixteen, was considered too old for the schoolroom, and was taken away to live with relatives; poor Jane
felt greatly deprived. 'It was a queer feeling to be, for the first
time, entirely on my own.'

Shortly, Mrs. Grant returned to England to fetch Elinor
back to Calcutta; and Jane was transferred to a small new
school at Bishopstoke, run by a couple of governesses, whom
Uncle Charles Plowden knew. Jane took to both of them, especially the French governess, and benefited greatly from her
instruction in the language and French classical literature.
'I took all the prizes the first year I was there; music, drawing,
French, English composition, good conduct. . . .' She stayed
there for two years, and it may have been then that she and her
brothers visited one of their Frere cousins, who had married
Christopher Wordsworth, then Canon of Westminster, in their
elegant London home. A story has persisted in the Strachey
family (and who else could have started it except Jane?) about
the Canon's unwitting humour in remonstrating with the
family cook, who, he discovered, had been making use of his
newfangled bathtub with running water, one of the first in
London: 'The worst of it is,' he said severely, 'that you have
been doing behind my back what you would not do before my
face.'

Once more, in 1856, Mrs. Grant came back to London, to
the Freres in Bedford Square, where Bartle, Jane's youngest
brother, was born in September. (Charles, the next to youngest,
was born in Calcutta in 1853.) After the school year was over in
1857, Jane went to live with her mother, the baby, Charles, and
her older brother Trevor at Haileybury, where Trevor was
supposed to be qualifying for the Indian Civil Service, but
obviously needed someone to sit over him and make him do his

homework and get up to go to chapel. The treatment worked, and he graduated.

Meanwhile, Elinor had been married out in Calcutta, in April 1857, to Sir James Colvile, a man many years her senior and a great favourite with Calcutta society. He was in the legal department of the government and was now Chief Justice. With Elinor's father, he had been responsible for the famous law, framed by Grant and pushed through its legislative stages chiefly by his efforts, which provided for the remarriage of Hindu widows. Now Grant and Colvile and a few others of like liberal persuasion were inducting Canning, the new Governor, into their plans and views. But before they could go further with the establishment of a truly progressive state in India, they had first to weather the fury of the Mutiny, brought on, ultimately, by the opposite, unenlightened attitudes of far too many in the lower ranks of government and the military.

At the height of the Mutiny in midsummer 1857, Grant asked for and was gladly given the appointment to proceed up the Ganges by boat and carriage to Benares and Allahabad, join forces with such men as his brother-in-law George Plowden at Nagpur, and exercise judgment and control over both Europeans and natives, and especially get the peasants back to their crops, lest there should be famine and pestilence added to civil war. It was an enormous and a dangerous task, lasting for several months, until in February 1858 Canning himself relieved Grant of the post at Allahabad, and Grant returned to become President of Council in Calcutta. Hitherto, he had been renowned as the best administrator at desk-work in the government, but now he had also shown his prowess in action and danger.

When he walked one night in February back into his house at No. 6 Park Street, between Chowringhee and Circular Road, Mrs. Grant, Trevor, and Janie, and presumably some of the other children too, were there to greet him, having just arrived from England. Trevor had not seen his father since he was a small child, and sat up in bed with a gruff 'Who the devil are you?' perhaps expecting it to be a sepoy marauder. People's nerves were understandably on edge. There had been the total eclipse of the sun in September 1857, which many in India took as a portent of the dissolution of the East India Company's

Raj; and a beautiful fiery comet repeated this omen a year later.

By the autumn of 1858, the Mutiny and its aftermath were largely over, and substantial changes had been effected in the British government of India. The hegemony of the East India Company was ended, after centuries of acting as almost a private government (though latterly as the agent of the British government), and power was transferred in London from the Board of Governors of the Company to a Council for India at Whitehall. Lady Canning, writing on September 14 from Allahabad, where she had joined her husband, said: 'The Proclamation of the Queen's Government is not come yet. We are prepared to have fireworks and a huge dinner in celebration of it, and at Calcutta Mr. Grant is to have an enormous ball in Government House, and fireworks for the natives. . . . It is a point of nicety to express proper and great joy without behaving in an unseemly way towards the poor old defunct Koompanee.' Perhaps it was that celebration that Jane was remembering when she wrote about her greatly admired hero, Sir James Outram: 'I remember once sitting next him at a State dinner in Calcutta, at which my father presided, given after a Grand Review. He said to me: "When I look at your father and see him without a decoration on his breast, I feel ashamed of all the stars with which I am covered." '

For the celebration, Trevor Grant, being the tallest, stood at the head of the line of Calcutta Volunteers, and Major Richard Strachey was responsible for the 'splendid illumination of Calcutta that night'—including lines of oil lamps rising to a great crown over the dome of Government House. Strachey had been working closely with J. P. Grant II for some time, both in Calcutta and during the Mutiny in Allahabad. He had become a close friend of the Grants since his brother John had married their niece Kate Batten, back in 1856. When Janie at school in England had heard that news, she had stared at 'the peculiar name', Strachey. Thinking back, in her memoirs, over the years of coping with it, she supposed that when St. Peter asked her name at the pearly gates, she would automatically respond, 'Strachey—S–T–R–A–C–H–E–Y'. But she did not meet Richard until the summer of 1858 at the Grants' summer home in Naini Tal, when he was on his way back to

Calcutta to his assignment in the Public Works Department. He and Jane were engaged by November, and their marriage took place on January 4, 1859.

Jane was then not quite nineteen years old, and Richard forty-one. This generation gap seems to have been the rule rather than the exception in marriages of Anglo-Indian families. But Richard had been married before, when he was in England for several years in the early 1850's, on leave from the Army for his health, and following his extraordinary botanical researches in the mountains of Tibet that first won for him a name among British scientists. Lady Strachey writes touchingly of her husband's first marriage: 'Just before leaving to return to India, Sir Richard married his first wife, Caroline Anne Bowles, the only daughter of her widowed mother who resided at Malvern. Poor Caroline met with a sad fate. A few months after her arrival in India, she was attacked with fever, which brought on premature confinement, of which she died, in 1855. I shall never forget the kindness of old Mrs. Bowles when my husband and I returned from India about six years after. Painful as it must have been to her, she asked us and our little baby to stay with her at Malvern, and treated us as though we might have been her own. I called my second little girl Caroline, but she died at the age of five months.'

Richard and Jane spent much of 1859 in the hills at Ootacamund, staying at a hotel, while they were expecting their first child and Richard was recovering from another bout of illness. They returned to Calcutta after the birth of Elinor, and Jane Strachey had the pleasure then of being herself the 'Burra Mem' of Calcutta society for a few weeks, her father having been made Lieutenant-Governor of Bengal on May 1, 1859, and her mother having returned to England. The Richard Stracheys and their infant daughter followed her in January 1860. It is pleasant to think of the Stracheys enjoying, however briefly, the splendours of the beautiful old government residency at Alipore, to which the Grants had moved, in view of the later architectural horrors at Lancaster Gate in London.

Mr. Grant, as Lieutenant-Governor, earned every penny of his increased salary. He had had to withstand years of obloquy from colleagues in India and Tory die-hards at home, being tarred with the same brush as 'Clemency Canning' for his liberal, just, and progressive measures. Once in 1857, Astley's in London had put on a play about the Mutiny, in which, so Lady Strachey recalled, 'My father was introduced. Of course we were all much interested . . . and my mother took a box at Astley's for all the family, including Charlie, who was then four years old. A scene came on: some military officers entered with five chained Indian prisoners, and awaited the arrival of the Civil Authority. He entered—a young man of about four-and-twenty in a white linen suit. As he did so, Charlie, who was in the front of the box, called out in a loud voice: "That's not my Papa!" to the amused astonishment of those around. The young man, after listening to the officers, addressed the prisoners thus:

‘ "Now air you guilty or air you not?"

'They threw up their hands: "No, upon our honour."

'Turning haughtily to the officers, the young man said:

‘ "In virtue of my 'igh hoffice, I release the prisoners!" ' and left the stage amidst the hisses and groans of the gallery.'

Still under the cloud of suspicion and ill-will, Grant was now in charge of the welfare of over seventy million people. With his usual patience, attention to facts, and concern for the long-range interests of the country, Grant performed the difficult business of adjusting the indigo farmers' complaints, pacifying the dacoits, or bandits, and accomplishing other legal and educational reforms. His term should have lasted five years, but because of ill health, he resigned in 1862. The tide, even in Bengal, had by now turned in his favour. He was celebrated and honoured by a great public meeting for all Calcutta and its suburbs on April 16, 1862, with a formal Resolution praising and congratulating him. The Queen bestowed upon him knighthood in the Order of the Bath, and there was some talk of his being selected to be the next Governor of Bombay. But he withdrew to London and private life, just at the time that the Richard Stracheys' leave was over and they were returning to duty in Calcutta.

Jane Strachey was now undergoing the same kind of life that her mother had led, while the children were coming along. Her life was divided between England and India, with two-year so-journs in the East in 1862-3, 1868-9, and 1877-8. Colvile had re-tired in 1859, and he and Elinor and their son had also returned to London, where he became a member of the Privy Council, on its judicial committee. His homes (Craigflower, in Fifeshire, and his town house in London, No. 8 Rutland Gate) and Sir J. P. Grant's home, first in London and then at Willenhall near Barnet, sheltered the Stracheys when they were in England. Lady Strachey remarks, 'When I had to leave Elinor and Dick behind me, the Colviles took them in, and I was thus spared one of the worst trials of most Anglo-Indian mothers, uncertainty as to the happiness of the children they have had to part with.' That would have been in 1868, for on the first of these trips to India, the Stracheys took their two eldest with them. Maybe they arrived in Calcutta in time to see the Grants as they were leaving for home. The hot weather had begun, and they headed for Simla in the hills. 'My children, Elinor and Dick, aged three years and under two, went with their nurse on an elephant. Richard and I, and my cousin, Nina Plowden, went in a carriage and pair.' Jane loved playing chaperone, as the married lady, to this favourite pretty cousin, who eventually became Lady Grey, and mother of Lady Eden, and grandmother of Lady Brooke.

Simla's climate was more like England's, and the life in what at first was a kind of summer camp was delightfully free and informal. In 1864, Simla was declared the summer capital, so that the higher officials of government could stay there with the women and small children. But in the summers of 1862 and 1863, Richard Strachey would have had to return to Calcutta once the family was established. The slow journey to and from the mountains, in a caravan of horses and carriages and elephants, servants, wagons, and pack animals, encamping every night in an Arabian Nights kind of luxury, was itself a pleasure.

Richard Strachey, now a colonel, was first acting secretary, then Secretary of the Department of Public Works in Calcutta, and also Consulting Engineer for Railways and first Inspector-General of Irrigation. He had to do a lot of travelling. For some twenty years in this part of his career he worked at his pet projects for the improvement of Indian economic life and civilization: the systematic extension of railways and canals, establishing adequate forest service, financing transportation and irrigation by special loans, and reorganizing the fiscal and administrative systems of Indian government to achieve efficient decentralization. In the latter part of this period, he was working hand in glove with his brother John Strachey, especially to stabilize the rupee and introduce proper financial and monetary reforms. Indeed as the century advanced there were periods when John and Richard Strachey between them were practically the governors of the whole country. Many a public works structure in India bore their name, and the great railway bridge at Agra named after Richard Strachey is still in use.

Jane Strachey, living with her children and assorted visiting youngsters at 'The Yarrows' in Simla, set herself to provide amusement with amateur theatricals, in an improvised summer theatre in the Assembly Rooms and sometimes in private performances at home. She had the help of several officers and their wives, and especially of Mr. and Mrs. William Tayler, friends of the Pattle ladies (Mr. Tayler had long ago constituted himself master of revels for Calcutta). They put on such plays as *Still Waters Run Deep* and *Betsy Baker* and *She Stoops to Conquer*. Besides, there were impromptu games of charades, and a sketching club, and dances; Jane excelled at waltzing. Once a leopard dashed through the veranda outside the drawing-room, where Jane was sitting with Nina, and Jane, without stopping to think, seized a croquet mallet and rushed after it. It wisely escaped.

Parcels of books were ordered from home, among them in 1863 the collected works of Robert Browning. Jane received these volumes 'as I was starting with the Viceroy's camp on the march to Simla. I opened them first as I sat on the hillside, and shall never forget the exquisite pleasure and enthusiastic admiration with which they filled me. I wrote a full account of it all to my sister, and received in reply a letter in which she said: "It was very fortunate I received your letter just when I did, as I happened, immediately afterwards, to meet Robert Browning at dinner, and should not have known anything about him but for that. I have seen him several times since." On reading this I sat down on the hearthrug and cried! However, I returned to England very shortly afterwards, and, of course, my sister, who was then well acquainted with him, introduced me to him. Our meeting was at the Saturday Popular Concert: my sister lent me her seat, which was immediately behind Browning and his son "Pen." He turned round and greeted me as Lady Colvile's sister. I have still my programme of that day's concert, on which I wrote:—

    ' "And did you once see Browning plain?
    And did he stop and speak to you?" '

From leopards to literary lions, from the stage to the nursery, and from Calcutta to London, Jane Strachey's life was amply exciting during the 1860's. In London, through Richard's family, she made the acquaintance of the Carlyles. She met George Eliot, and Lewes, and became a regular visitor at their Sunday afternoons; her friendship with George Eliot was more than a formal acquaintance; they shared a passion for the theatre and often met each other at plays and concerts. Jane never got over the gratification of Lewes's compliment that he thought her just like Dorothea in *Middlemarch*.

In 1865, Richard Strachey resigned and came home to England to stay, but the failure of the Bank of Agra in 1866, into which he had put all his and his brothers' funds in the effort to build it up into a Bank of India, forced him to return for another five-year term. The Stracheys had rented a house in a back street in Lancaster Gate, but this they gave up and went to the Grants. Then Sir J. P. Grant II was drafted by the government to take over Jamaica, which was in a state of turmoil. Lady Grant, not wanting to accompany him there, joined Jane and the children to go and live near their relatives in Edinburgh; Jane rented No. 32 St. George's Square, a house that had belonged to Sir Walter Scott's family, and Lady Grant lived somewhere nearby. The baby Dorothy, born in 1866, had now been added to little Elinor and Richard. They all paid visits occasionally that year to Craigflower and Rothiemurchus, and Jane had a good time making new friends in Scotland. She enthusiastically circulated the first petition to Parliament for votes for women, securing quantities of signatures, which petition was presented to Parliament in 1868 by J. S. Mill himself. Jane had read *On Liberty* in 1859 and had thereafter been a fervent disciple of Mill.

Jane returned to India in 1868 to join Richard, leaving the two older children behind with the Colviles, and taking little Dorothy with her; Dorothy's début in Calcutta society occurred at the age of three as a bridesmaid to the daughter of the Vice-roy, Sir John Lawrence. Another son, Ralph, was born to the Stracheys during this two-year visit, and presumably returned to England with his mother in 1869, to stay again with the Colviles in Scotland and London. Lady Grant and Jane spent the winter of 1870–1 in Florence, where Richard Strachey joined them at the end of his five years of service in India. It was on that visit to Italy that Lady Strachey first made the acquaintance of Marie Souvestre, who had to close her school in Fontainebleau when the Germans invaded Paris in the Franco-Prussian War. 'She fell in love with' Jane Strachey 'at once, and a friendship began which lasted till the end of her life, in 1905'. Through Marie, Jane met many interesting Europeans, during that winter and on many later occasions while visiting her in Paris; and the story is well known of how Lady Strachey helped Marie Souvestre transfer her school for girls to Wimbledon near London, where the Strachey and the Ritchie children and many others of their connections studied, and some even became teachers.

In 1872, the Stracheys, now back in London to stay, Richard having retired again from active service in India, bought a fine old house on Clapham Common, which they named Stowey House after the village near the Stracheys' country seat. They lived there for twelve years until they moved to No. 69 Lancaster Gate, north of Hyde Park in town. When they moved into Stowey House, Jane 'was then thirty-two, and this was the first time in my life that I had ever spent more than two years in the same house. I bought a good deal of furniture at auctions, which I much enjoyed going to. It was before the days when Sheraton became so fashionable, and I bought a really beautiful table of his. . . . I paid 18 pounds for it, and when, forty-seven years afterwards, I had to sell it, it went for 300 pounds.' It has been customary to complain of Lady Strachey's tastelessness in furnishings and eccentricity in dress, but a combination of causes may have produced these effects, such as lack of funds, and years of living out of trunks in furnished lodgings.

Pippa, Oliver, and Pernel Strachey were born at Stowey House, at intervals of two years, and then came another period of long absences from home. The first journey was to

America, Richard and Jane accompanying Joseph Hooker, who had long been a close friend and colleague in botanical and other scientific interests. Hooker and the Stracheys joined Professor Asa Gray and his wife in Boston, July 8, 1877, after a ten-day voyage on the *Parthia*.

In Boston, Jane and Mrs. Gray got acquainted (they had a love of music and poetry in common) and perhaps did some sightseeing, while the men visited 'with Professor Sargent, curator of the Botanical Garden at Harvard and of a magnificent park, the Arnold Arboretum, which was not yet laid out, but was to be the Kew of Boston'. They also took in the Museum and the Peabody Institute in Salem, and Wellesley College, 'a rich man's gift to the State for the education of female school teachers. . . .' Then Hooker, the Grays, and the Stracheys set out to join Professor Hayden, as part of the botanical wing of the official surveying party then at work in Colorado, Utah, Nevada, and California. They took the paddle steamer from Boston to New York, picking up another botanist named Thurber at Providence. He gave them a swift tour of New York in the two hours before their train left. Boston, Lady Strachey recalled, was a perfectly charming town; but New York, according to Hooker, was too much like Liverpool. 'The railway journeys were long and desperately hot'—to Cincinnati, for an overnight stop, and thence to St. Louis, where the rest of the botanical party met them, Dr. Lambourne, Professor Leidy and his wife and daughter, Dr. Hayden, and Capt. Stevenson, his assistant. Then they rode for 'two nights and nearly two days on the newly made railway to Pueblo across the prairies along the Arkansas River'. Once in Colorado, some of the party went north, and some south, to spread their explorations at different latitudes and temperatures and elevations among the Rockies. The Stracheys and Hooker drove two days to La Veta Pass, where the Grays and Hayden joined them, coming by rail, and they pitched their five tents just over the pass on July 23.

From La Veta, after the Stracheys had made a side trip down to Mexico (i.e. probably what is now New Mexico), they all proceeded to Colorado Springs, where they climbed Pike's Peak, and then to Denver and Salt Lake City by train and on to Ogden. At each principal stop, they stayed to allow the botanists to fan out on their surveying and collecting excursions.

Lady Strachey says she loved camping in the mountains, 'though
I must say that after my experience of the Himalayas, the
Rockies seemed somewhat diminutive'. Sometimes they stayed
in hotels in little mining 'cities'—of about fifty houses. Hooker
was much impressed: 'Here at . . . the extreme finger-end of
civilisation the streets are watered better than at Kew, people
sleep without locks to their doors, the fire-engines are well
manned and in capital order, and of food there is *no end* . . . all
is brought up by train from Denver. . . . At Hotels . . . the food
is most abundant, wastefully so, and I do not like the little messes
of endless meats, breadstuffs, and vegetables that are served
to each at all meals. Each individual is surrounded by a con-
stellation of little thick white plates, which the waiters throw
down and about like quoits, making a *dreadful* clatter. . . .'
The high scale of living, the cleanliness, and the free-handed
lynch laws impressed them all.

At Salt Lake City, the party was permitted to call on
Brigham Young, 'and a curious visit it was too', recalled Lady
Strachey. 'We sat around, at first, in complete silence, until
the opening ceremony of presenting each guest with a tumbler
of cold water was performed. Brigham Young was in person exactly like the type of a long established family butler. A curious
thing about him that I remarked, was that he never looked anyone
in the face. I was determined to catch sight of his eyes, and so
held my own down when he approached and stood over me with
the tumbler of water; then I suddenly lifted mine up, and encountered the full gaze of his, which were far from being [those]
of a family butler; they showed great intelligence, power, and
inflexible will.'

When the party reached Ogden, the Stracheys decided to
return to England before they had intended, and so they never
got to California. News had arrived of the children's illness
—but that proved to have been less serious than supposed—
and besides, Richard would have to go back to India on government business, including the Famine Commission. They had
been at home in London again only a short time before they
set out for the East, taking Elinor and Dorothy with them.
Then John Strachey had to come home from India to have his
eyesight attended to, and Richard and Jane stayed on, while
Richard took over his brother's duties as Finance Member of

the Supreme Council. This was the last of Jane's two-year sojourns in India. She found the society much changed since the 1860's, but as usual she enjoyed the social pleasures, especially getting to know Lord Robert Lytton and his family, in Simla. He and Leslie Stephen's brother, Sir James Fitzjames Stephen, were close friends of John Strachey. Elinor, the Richard Stracheys' eldest child, was now through school at Fontainebleau and of marriageable years. Dorothy was the same age as Betty Lytton and enjoyed her company as playmate —Jane must have been reminded by those two of her own first visit to India in 1852. When Jane left India in 1879 to return to London, it was for the last time, though of course her contacts with Indian affairs continued through Richard's increasingly responsible positions in government and the East India Railway Company. Besides, their three eldest sons also had careers in India.

To complete this great Victorian family, three more children were born during the 1880's, Lytton, Marjorie, and James. The family had moved to Lancaster Gate before James came along, and his eldest sister, Elinor, now Mrs. James Rendel, was herself the mother of children older than this littlest brother. One's mind boggles thinking of the armies of servants, from Indian ayahs, wet nurses, laundresses, governesses, and parlour-maids, to butlers, who made possible the support of such a family, allowing its mistress time not only for close attention to her children, their health, and their education, but also to write books, and to roam off on excursions, sometimes to Europe, and again in 1884 to Washington, D.C., accompanying her husband to the Prime Meridian Conference, and in the summers to move the entire family to Rothiemurchus or to rented houses in the home counties.

Jane Strachey had now reached the heyday of life, 'the golden years' of fulfilment. For a splendid account of this period, I refer the reader to Betty Askwith's chapters on the Strachey family, in *Two Victorian Families*, mentioned above. I will attempt only to round out the story of Lady Strachey's life with matters that lie more or less outside the theme and period of Miss Askwith's work.

During the 1880's and 1890's, Lady Strachey began to publish some of her writings. These, to begin with, grew out of her informal teaching of her children and their classmates, encouraging them to write poems and reading aloud to them. 'All my children,' she wrote, 'had a great taste and some capacity for literature, music, and acting, which I greatly enjoyed doing my best to develop. In quite early days I started a weekly magazine, to which everyone was expected to contribute. I wrote a leading political article, and we had a Meeting of Parliament once a week, at which the week's magazine was read aloud. Upon one of these occasions, Ralph, the youngest present, about four, had to be committed to the Tower for persisting in creating a disturbance in Parliament! We continued for many years to write occasional verses, of which I eventually made a collection, and had them typed and bound together, under the title of "Our Rhymes: or Five Minutes with the Worst Authors." '

Lady Strachey's first published book was entitled *Lay Texts for the Young in English and French* (1887), a calendar of maxims, intended to benefit adolescent schoolchildren. This was followed by *Nursery Lyrics* (1893), some of which were later set to music by her son Oliver; they are sentimental and humorous, sometimes patently autobiographical. A second edition of *Nursery Lyrics*, published by Chatto & Windus in 1922, contains several new poems and the text of the playlet 'Little Boy Blue'. One of the new poems, several stanzas long, an invocation to the 'Muse of infant song', prefaces this edition; its opening lines suggest the quality of the work:

> The feathery dandelion weed
> Blown straight at Shakespeare's bosom,
> Sprang up a crop of Mustard-seed,
> Moth, Cobweb, and Peasblossom.
> You whistled into Drayton's ear,
> To which his fancy dancing,
> Pigwiggin, Oberon, appear,
> And the proud Emmet prancing.

Next came an anthology of selections from English poetry whose title, *Poets on Poets* (1894), is descriptive of its theme. Lady Strachey's eight-page introduction to these passages from Chaucer to Tennyson is the best sample of her prose style in print, intellectually forceful, direct and economical, but marked by extended figures of speech, a very different style from the rambling informality of her memoirs.

In 1893, her father died, and her eldest brother, John Peter Grant III, took over as laird of Rothiemurchus. Walter Seton-Kerr, her father's former assistant in Calcutta, undertook to write a biography of him, which was published in 1899, in the preface of which Jane Strachey is thanked 'for access to Grant's correspondence, and for many valuable suggestions and hints. . . .' Perhaps it was this biographical research that started her on preparing another family memoir for publication, the very interesting book by her aunt Eliza Grant Smith, *Memoirs of a Highland Lady*, published by John Murray in 1898. Jane selected the first and longest portion of this work, which had been privately printed and circulated widely in the family, and in her preface she gave a summary of the latter portion of Mrs. Smith's life. (She had died in 1885.) Perhaps, to speculate still more widely, acquaintance with James Russell Lowell during his residence in London in the 1880's might have promoted the Strachey family's interest in Mrs. Smith's *Memoirs*. The Lowell family had had a long connection with the Grants, having known Jane's great-grandmother, Anne Grant of Laggan, in the early nineteenth century in Edinburgh. She was the author of *Memoirs of an American Lady* and *Letters from the Highlands*, both best-sellers. But this is to stray back into the era of the Clapham Sect, and since Lady Strachey says nothing in her memoirs of knowing Mr. Lowell, and seems not to have maintained her earlier contact with Boston, the speculation is probably invalid, except as an example of the curious intertwining between Clapham and Bloomsbury.

Jane Strachey's verse style is a little more distinguished than her prose; it testifies to her strong sense of rhythm and her ear-mindedness. Trouble with her eyesight may have encouraged her reliance on sound and her phenomenal ability to memorize verse; she knew, for example, long passages of Milton by heart and once, at the age of eighty-four, recited *Lycidas* entire to Leonard and Virginia Woolf. She was very short-sighted and often refused to wear her spectacles, especially when having her photograph taken, lest the picture would not show her beautiful forget-me-not blue eyes at their best. When she was visiting her daughter Dorothy Bussy in Roquebrune on the Riviera in the in winter of 1915–16, she had her first severe attack of trouble in the left eye, for which she underwent a miserable hospitalization in Paris, then a long recuperation which did not succeed, and finally had to have the eye removed in hospital in London, July 1917. (This was the occasion when Oxford Circus, in the near neighbourhood of the hospital, was bombed, and Lady Strachey, getting over the operation, had to wait in the bomb shelter with the other patients, mostly wounded soldiers, and startled the doctor in charge by calmly smoking a cigarette; he said he wished the Kaiser could see her then—it would make him despair of victory.)

One of her poems, entitled *Forestalled*, will serve to exemplify her talent for verse, and also to demonstrate how much she lived in the world of sounds:

> Up the pallid arch of heaven sprang the golden horses,
>> beating
> With their crystal hoofs a pathway for the day,
> All the air broke into colour, dewy-cool, and gay with
>> greeting
> From the myriad forces waking into play;
> Then the rapture of the morning through all my pulses
>> swinging,
> Would have sung itself aloud in paeans high;
> But I could not breathe the music that in my heart was
>> ringing,
> For the singing of the skylark in the sky.
>
> In the glory of the noontide, the summer-world outshining
> With its pomp of purple roses and the rest,
> Seemed in palpitating stillness, perfection's self divining,
> To hang one breathless moment at its best;
> And rhythmically through my blood the happy tunes were
>> thrumming,
> As lazily I sunned me on the lea;
> But I could not catch the melody that lingered in its
>> coming,
> For the humming in the foxglove of the bee.

Day's splendour had departed, all the colour and the riot
    That filled the frolic hours as they sped;
And melancholy evening came footing soft and quiet
    With a garland of remembrance for my head;
There was freedom now from effort, there was respite from
        pursuing,
    Joy was over, yet I knew that calm was good;
But I could not chant the low-toned lay where patience
        chides at rueing,
    For the cooing of the ring-dove in the wood.

Then the darkling heavens deepened up to zone on zone
        supernal,
    Where silently the countless hosts of stars
Stood visible as witnesses mysterious and eternal
    Of man's spirit beating vainly at the bars;
And fancy and desire yearned on mocking visions, paling
    In the lustre of those worlds of alien light,
But I could not fling abroad my cry of passion unavailing,
    For the wailing of the nightingale at night.

Perhaps this lyric should better have been entitled *Frustrated*.
Yet falling short of poetic excellence as it does, it nevertheless
provides a side-light on its author's being that is most disarming.

The turn of the century ended an era in the Strachey family
life. The youngest of the children was now launched into the
world. Sir Richard had resigned one after the other from his
numerous committees and finally, in 1907, owing to his
increasing deafness, from the chairmanship of the East India
Railways. With a consequent diminished income, and with a
smaller family under the roof, the Stracheys moved from
Lancaster Gate to No. 67 Belsize Park Gardens in Hampstead.
There Sir Richard died, full of honours, at the ripe age of ninety-
one, on February 12, 1908, only two months after the death
of his brother, Sir John. For Lady Strachey it was the narrow
thread in the hour-glass when the past dwindled to a point,
beyond which it would widen again into a gathering future. She
was still vigorous in her sixties, and her interests, intellectual
and social, included the keenest delight in the successes of her
children.

One absorbing interest continued to be the cause of Women's Suffrage. In England, the Suffrage Movement was divided into four departments of work for the freedom of women: in education, in securing an equal moral standard between men and women, in liberating women to take part in industry and the professions, and in obtaining equal political status. By the turn of the century, the last of these four objects predominated, and the various councils in different centres of Great Britain had amalgamated into the National Union of Women's Suffrage Societies. Lady Strachey sat on the executive committee of the N.U.W.S.S. for many years, representing Cambridge, and aided the work especially by writing a number of the pamphlets propagandizing for votes for women. One of these, No. 51, *Reduced to the Absurd*, by Lady Strachey, . . . Price One Penny, is a series of syllogisms showing her brand of wit, some rather heavy-handed, some hilarious; for example:

'Queen Victoria did not know what it was like to be politi-
    cally impotent.
Queen Victoria would have strenuously opposed Women's
    Suffrage.
Therefore women must go without it.
Blind men do not know what it is like to be short-sighted.
Blind men are strenuously opposed to spending money on
    spectacles.
Therefore short-sighted school-children must go without
    spectacles.'

'A woman's sphere is home.
Therefore she should never go out of it.
A man's sphere is not home.
Therefore he should never go into it.'

The series, published between 1907 and 1909, lists the common objections to women's suffrage. One of these and its answer, appearing in two of Lady Strachey's pamphlets, provide an interesting background to Virginia Woolf's thought in her well-known feminist essay *A Room of One's Own*. The Objection, No. 4, reads: 'There has never been a woman so great as the greatest men. There is no female Shakespeare or Newton, so the sex is too intellectually feeble to have a vote.' To which Lady

Strachey replied: 'But votes are not given as competition prizes. . . . It does not seem reasonable to a sweated work-woman to be told that if she wants to be listened to she should have written King Lear. To be sure, Tom Smith did not write it either, and yet *he* has a vote.

'Women think that without *them* there would have been no Shakespeare or Newton; and that perhaps if women were raised a bit, and allowed to use what powers of intellect they have, there might be more intellectual giants produced. At present, in proportion to the race, their number is very small indeed.'

One interesting argument for women's suffrage, not dealt with by Lady Strachey, but on which she could well have spoken, was the fact that for generations before 1857, women stockholders in the East India Company, of whom there were a great many, had voted to elect the Company's Court of Directors, who were the government of India, that important part of the British Empire; but these same women could not vote for members of Parliament. India was also brought into the debate by those opposed to women's suffrage with the objection that since Indian women had so little liberty, it would be a scandal to them if British women were enfranchised. On this Lady Strachey spoke her mind, like her father's daughter, in a vigorous letter to *The Times*: ' . . . the loyalty and contentment of our Indian fellow-subjects depend not at all on the basis of our Government in England, but on how the Government deals with them in their own country: on the wisdom with which we there respect ideals of life altogether contrary to our own, wherever it is possible to do so without outraging justice and humanity.'

As the movement progressed, it became customary, from 1907 on, to hold an annual demonstration march in London, culminating in a mass political meeting in Queen's Hall or the Albert Hall. The N.U.W.S.S. joined sometimes with the militant suffrage wing in these marches, which were increasingly spectacular with floats and bands and flags. The first one, February 9, 1907, known as the Mud March, from the state of the weather, was organized by Miss Philippa Strachey, and headed by Dame Millicent Fawcett with Lady Strachey and Lady Balfour marching beside her; other Strachey daughters and their friends participated, Pippa not allowing a single one of their acquaintance, male or female, to go without some assigned job in facilitating the march. The procession gathered in Hyde Park, went down Pall Mall, and stopped at Exeter Hall in the Strand, where John Maynard Keynes, then an undergraduate and staying with the Stracheys at Lancaster Gate, was detailed to open the Hall—he had to find the key first, which had been hidden by enemies—and keep out the hecklers until all the marchers had been seated. Lady Strachey also participated in the first great united march of 1908, fifteen thousand strong, 'walking, tall and stately, at the head of the procession'. Behind her floated among other banners one reading: 'Non angeli, sed anglae'. When at last the Representation of the People Act had been passed and suffrage had been won, Lady Strachey had the pleasure of attending the great celebration meeting, organized by the Council of the N.U.W.S.S., at the Queen's Hall, on March 13, 1918, which happened to be her seventy-eighth birthday and the fiftieth anniversary of the movement inaugurated by the petition which she had signed so long ago in Edinburgh. Some of her songs, set to well-known tunes—e.g. 'Auld Lang Syne'—and published in the *Women's Suffrage Songbook* used at these rallies, were sung on that occasion. As a sample, one might cite stanza three of 'By-and-Bye' to the tune of 'Come Lasses and Lads':

> 'Says Sue, I'm true blue, and pray what are you?
>> I'm red as a poppy, says Nan.
> Ould Oirland for me, says Norah Machree,
>> And Poll's for the Labour man.
> Then every lass steps out
>> For what she most requires,
> And puts her cross to her favourite boss
>> Just as her heart desires.'

At the age of seventy-eight, one should be allowed to retire from active business and rest on the satisfying laurels of having been one of the leaders in the army that achieved enfranchisement for the women of Great Britain. The Great War was now over. The children were doing well. Lytton was basking in new eminence as the author of *Eminent Victorians*. In 1919, Lady Strachey and her daughters Pippa and Marjorie moved to No. 51 Gordon Square, a tall row house on the east side of the square, right in the heart of the emerging Bloomsbury Group's homes. Here Lady Strachey settled down to write her memoirs, just as the inner circle of the group was forming its own Memoir Club.

The younger generation would not, of course, rest content with the achievements of its forebears. Rights for women at the polls, for example, was only a superficial change; Bloomsbury feminism, as Quentin Bell clearly explains, was more profound and far-reaching. Lady Strachey, who had been a conveyor to her family and their friends, not only of feminism and political liberalism, but also of that feeling of kinship through alliances of clans and colleagues stretching back over generations, was now herself only an eminent Victorian. But her powerful influence may be measured by the devotion of the younger generation to their sense of living history, of which she was to them a symbol.

Mrs. Woolf, in the tribute quoted at the beginning of this chapter, says that as Lady Strachey grew older, her memory of that past grew more distinct. She lost her eyesight 'almost entirely some years before she died. She could no longer go foraging and triumphing through English literature—for it seemed as if she carried on even the passive act of reading with something of the vigour with which she strode the streets, peering forward with her short-sighted eyes, or tossed her head high in a shout of laughter. But she could talk, she could argue, she could join in the disputes of the younger generation. . . . Her mind was still busy with literature, still active with suggestions for reviving forgotten plays, for editing old texts, for bringing to light some hidden splendour in those old books which she . . . almost commanded the younger generation to love as she had loved them.'

In the summer of 1928, 'though too weak to walk any more, she sat on her balcony and showered down upon the faces that she could not see a vast maternal benediction. It was as if the Victorian age in its ripeness, its width, with all its memories and achievements behind it were bestowing its blessing. And we should be blind indeed if we did not wave back to her a salute full of homage and affection.'

5

Anne Isabella Ritchie, née Thackeray
(1837–1919)

AUNT ANNY, as Lady Ritchie was known to the Bloomsbury
Group, and her niece Mary Warre-Cornish (who married
Desmond MacCarthy, and who will be the subject of the next
chapter), represent the more conservative and religiously
orthodox, though still liberally feministic influences on the
Group. They brought into the family backgrounds of Bloomsbury, in addition to the tribes of Stephens, Pattles, Stracheys, and
Grants, two more great Anglo-Indian families, the Thackerays
and the Ritchies.

The relationships are somewhat complex. Anne Thackeray's
husband, Sir Richmond Ritchie, was also her second cousin. Her
father, the novelist, was a first cousin of Judge William Ritchie
of Calcutta (Richmond Ritchie's father); Thackeray passed
some of his childhood in London with his aunt and uncle,
William Ritchie's parents. Then, through the marriage of
Harriet Marion Thackeray, that is 'Minny', Anne's younger
sister, to Leslie Stephen as his first wife, Anne became eventually Aunt Anny to the young Stephens. She was also a great
friend of Sir James and Elinor Grant Colvile and of Sir Richard
and Lady Strachey, and godmother to their youngest, James
Strachey. Mary Warre-Cornish MacCarthy was a grand-
daughter of William Ritchie, and thus also a niece of Uncle
Richmond and Aunt Anny, whom she used to visit frequently
in London and the Isle of Wight.

But when one looks at the bewildering family relations of
these tribes, it becomes evident that more than kinship by blood
or marriage would be needed to consider any member of the
older generation as a genuine 'background' of the Bloomsbury
Group. Common interests and special affections would have
to prevail, and Aunt Anny qualifies partly because of her
singular distinction in her own person and as a writer, and
partly because of her position as the familiar friend of practi-

cally everybody who was anybody in the literary and artistic world of the Victorian era. True, Bloomsbury was rebelling against the Victorian world, but it was also rooted in it and unable to escape wholly being the transmitters of its traditions and its legacies from a remoter past. To them, Aunt Anny, like Lady Strachey, though so different from her, was an epitome of that world.

Comparatively little has appeared recently in print about Anne Thackeray Ritchie, and this is a pity, for she is well worth knowing and should not be forgotten. Her daughter, Mrs. Fuller, with the aid of Violet Hammersley, brought out a charming anthology of Lady Ritchie's memoirs and letters under the title *Thackeray's Daughter*, in 1951. There are also several amusing passages about her in Noel Annan's distinguished book on Leslie Stephen, published the same year. And Gordon Ray's biography of Thackeray gives hitherto unpublished material on Anny's life up to 1863.

But aside from these, there has been no republishing of her works, nothing since a selection of her letters, in 1924, and very few further words about her in print. Is she indeed now nothing but a museum piece, a historical footnote to her father's works and career? Of her ten books of fiction, most of them novels of 'domestic fiction', published between 1863 and 1887, the best compare favourably with some of her father's, in my opinion. Like his, and like the early Bloomsbury fiction, they build on the persons, scenes, and events of the real life surrounding the author, transforming and adapting these factual realities into stories, which suffer, however, from too much random material, editorializing, and moralizing, not palatable to modern taste in fiction. The same might be said of her father's and of other Victorian novelists' work. Virginia Woolf leniently excused her aunt's over-copious pen by reminding us that there is such a thing as atmosphere; but Mrs. Woolf herself taught us to expect that an atmospheric build-up should be thoroughly integrated and never obtrusive as such. She reports that Leslie Stephen had greatly admired his sister-in-law Anny's novels for their 'perception, humour, [and] mere delicate and tender and beautiful emotion', but had deplored their lack of the 'clearness, proportion, and neatness' to be found in Jane Austen's novels.

The latter part of Anne Thackeray Ritchie's career as a writer was occupied exclusively with memoirs, a type of composition in which she excelled brilliantly. From the biographical introductions to Thackeray's complete works, in the edition of 1898, revised and enlarged in 1911, to the posthumously published collection *From Friend to Friend* (1919), she contributed some seven volumes of these familiar essays, on subjects ranging from Chopin and George Sand to Browning and Mrs. Oliphant. The famous subjects, as in the case of her memoirs of W. M. Thackeray, are presented almost invariably from the author's personal point of view, mingling her own experience with her subject's and conveying her own delighted, keen-eyed observation. She takes the reader into the world of her memories to share the humour, the surprises, the discernments and the inspirations of her alert, poetic sensibility. Virginia Woolf, writing an obituary appreciation of her in *The Times Literary Supplement*, March 6, 1919, praises the memoir sketches very highly, claiming that in them Lady Ritchie almost 'invented an art of her own . . . exquisitely inspired'. Those who wish a clear living picture of the Victorians will go to them rather than to 'stout official biographies'. It is in these memoirs that one can both become best acquainted with Lady Ritchie and her world and also see her possible literary influence on the younger generation of Bloomsbury, who were themselves all memoir writers at one time or another.

The facts of Lady Ritchie's life are summarized dryly and superficially in the few paragraphs appended to her husband's biography in the *D.N.B.* and in a list of dates contained in *Thackeray's Daughter*. They might be reviewed here as background to a sketch of her character. Nancy Lewis, writing of *Thackeray's Daughter*, makes a very perceptive remark: that for all the sunniness and Victorian conventionality of the view of life in her fiction, Lady Ritchie's own life was marked by disturbances, troubles and sorrows, and the unusual, not to say the unconventional. If she had not had an uncommonly buoyant, optimistic temperament, she could hardly have survived so graciously the blows that fortune dealt her.

She was the first child of the happy but short-lived marriage of Thackeray and Isabella Shawe. Born on June 9, 1837, in London, and brought up in the neighbourhood of Russell

Square, Anne and her younger sister Minny were soon left motherless, when it became necessary for Mrs. Thackeray to live apart from her family in the country. The children were sent to Paris, to Thackeray's parents, the Carmichael-Smyths, when Anne was three and Minny one, and lived there until 1846. Reinforced by two later sojourns with their grand-parents in Paris, while Thackeray was lecturing in America in the 'fifties, this French experience made Anne bi-lingual and almost bi-national, as was often the case with Anglo-Indian children to whom Paris and London were almost equally home.

Anne was deeply devoted to her father. The girls came back to live with him in the Kensington Square neighbourhood and shared his rapid rise to fame and comparative wealth, his friends, even some of his travels on the Continent. They were educated by a succession of governesses and tutors at home and by Thackeray himself. Under his wise and light-handed governance, Anne cultivated her literary gifts and made her début as a fiction writer in the *Cornhill Magazine* in 1860, under his editorship. He also introduced the girls to society; his friends became their friends. The blow of his unexpected death on Christmas Eve in 1863 would have shattered their world, had it not been for the kindness and love of these friends.

The sisters made a new home together in the same Kensington Square neighbourhood, and after a few years were joined by Leslie Stephen, who married Minny in June 1867. This *ménage à trois*, with two writers of such different temperament working under the same roof, was kept in balance by Minny; but her death in childbirth in 1875 left them desolate. They stuck to-gether, however, until Stephen's remarriage, Anny's help being more than ever needed with the gradual discovery that little Laura Stephen was mentally deficient. That child eventually had also to be sent away to a home in the country; to the end of her life, Anne devoted countless excursions to visiting her mother, Isabella Shawe Thackeray, who died peacefully in 1894, and Laura Stephen, who survived her aunt until 1945.

Meanwhile, to Stephen's irritation over Anny's charming and constant chatter, her extravagance and her wayward mind ('her Irishness', as he called it, since her mother was of Irish descent), was added alarm over her affair with her much younger cousin, Richmond Ritchie. Ritchie is said to have begun to propose marriage to Anny, seventeen years his senior, while he was still at Eton. Their wedding in 1877, which shocked all their connections but made them both very happy, took Anny for a while out of the Stephen orbit. But after the death in 1895 of Leslie Stephen's second wife, Julia, Stephen turned to her again and used to visit her 'with clock-like regularity . . . once a week. During his last illness, . . . she paid him constant visits never minding the jeremiads and invectives he poured into her sympathetic ear. The story goes that on one occasion Anny took the initiative; came in brightly, sat down beside him and said, "Well Leslie—Damn—Damn—DAMN!" which made him burst out laughing and the visit was much gayer than usual.' Stephen called himself 'a gorilla' to Anny's 'dove'.

Richmond Ritchie's career in government, devoted to Indian affairs, proceeded steadily in importance and brilliance, while his wife's position as a distinguished popular writer and leader in literary and artistic society advanced correspondingly. They lived for a while in Wimbledon, but eventually in the Chelsea neighbourhood in London, and they rejoiced in two children, Hester and William ('Billy'). After Billy's marriage to Margaret Booth in 1906, there were also grandchildren, to whom some of Lady Ritchie's most delightful letters are addressed.

There were serious illnesses: Richmond Ritchie's from overwork, for recovery from which they lived for a while in St. Ives in the Stephens' house; Anny's thyroid trouble, from which after a serious operation she recovered. There were social triumphs: Sunday evening supper parties of literati in the St. George's Square home. There were literary triumphs: for Anny, the Fellowship in the Royal Society of Literature in 1903, the tremendous garden-party celebration of the Centennial Edition of Thackeray's works in 1911, the presidency of the English Association in 1912–13. And the knighthood for Richmond Ritchie was conferred in 1907, while Anny was enjoying a tour of Norway.

The comparatively early death of her husband in October 1912, and the hardships and heartaches of the First World War were the final blows of fortune to Anne Thackeray Ritchie. But she survived the war in sufficient health to enjoy a final few months at 'The Porch', the cottage on the Isle of Wight near

the Camerons and Tennysons, whither she and Minny had
retreated after their father's death so long ago. She even voted,
with characteristic vagueness, in the December 1918 elec-
tions, the first occasion after the enfranchisement of women in
Britain.

Some wonderful characterizations of Anny's mercurial temperament may be gathered from her *Letters*, that give intimate
glimpses of her as a child and a restless adolescent. Thackeray quotes from his mother's letter, in 1846, while she was
making preparations to bring the children home to him from
Paris: 'I assure you Nanny wants a firmer hand than mine. She
fights every inch of her way—if it's only to wash her face or
put on her stockings she will not do it without an argument.—
She is so clever, so selfish; so generous; so tender-hearted yet
so careless of giving pain.' Thackeray concludes: 'I am afraid
very much she is going to be a man of genius.' (P. 21.) Two
years later in London, Anny, aged ten, writes to her young
friend Letitia Cole about the 'honble. board of Juveniles', a
scheme occasioned by the European revolutions of 1848, to
solicit money for the 'stoppation of starvation'; she signs this
remarkable business letter 'A. Thanakins Titmarsh'. (Pp. 25–6.)

Her diaries for 1854–6 reflect the troubled restlessness of the
brilliant girl in a mid-Victorian world. At seventeen, she finds
that the whole world revolves for her around herself and
wonders whether everybody else has this same egocentric
experience. (Pp. 64–5.) At eighteen, she has just been reading
Mme. D'Arblay and is fired with ambition to record the great
in a 'Pepysina' of her own life and times; Carlyle shall be Dr.
Johnson, and her father shall be Goldsmith. 'I care for too many
things ever to do one perfectly. At one moment I'm mad to be
an artist, the next I languish for an author's fame, the third, I
would be mistress of German, and the fourth practise five hours
a day at the pianoforte.' (P. 72.) Anticipating her twentieth
birthday, she writes: 'Minny has been telling me how cross I
am getting sometimes. Twenty isn't a great deal but things
seem to pierce through and through my brain somehow, to get
inside my head and remain there jangling. I wonder if it is
having nothing to do all day pottering about with no particular
object? It is no use writing novels they are so stupid, it's no use
drawing little pictures, what's the good of them? Reading

Algebra is no use, I can't understand it. It's the same with Astronomy and I mingle them all up together. I often think how pleasant it would be to have no brains, only good honest well defined bodily labour.' (P. 96.) She goes on to describe briefly her nightmares, her nervous tension, and her fancies of illness. But the restless ambition continued to trouble her. In 1859, at a dinner at Mrs. Brookfield's, she talked with the Rt. Hon. Sir William Harcourt, who 'said aggravating things about women as usual. It's absurd to be annoyed as it's only a joke but it's very riling. O ye heavens! look at him and then look at me! Why am I to be contemptible all my days long?—Why is he to be so much more worth in his own, in everybody else's estimation? Why has he got work and leisure and strength and height and a thousand more advantages which I can't get at, not if I try till I burst like the frog in the fable. Why am I ridiculous when I spar at him with foolish little thrusts, I'm sure my brains are as good as his. I could feel this last night while I was listening to his talk with Mr. Brookfield.' (Pp. 109–10.)

This darker and more troubled side of her character was more noticeable to her, probably, than to others, even in her immediate family. Her father described her in 1855 as 'a perfect well-spring of happiness in herself'. (P. 70.) And her satiric humour, dry and sly, and directed against herself as well as the rest of the world, was early evident. It is very much like her father's, and it provides in her fiction the needed astringency and acidity to counteract a sometimes rather syrupy sweetness of sentiment. Like her father's it is a pervasive spirit, hard to isolate or to cite in quotation; it comes out, like his, not only in language but in the Thackerayan pen-and-ink sketches that adorn her letters. A typical instance, perhaps, is the conclusion of Chapter IV in *Chapters From Some Memoirs*, on 'My Professor of History', the eccentric little French teacher, who gave away all the carefully sacrificed gift of money which Anne had sent her to save her from starvation during the 1870 siege of Paris, gave it away to help buy some cannon for the defence of the arrondissement; Anne's conclusion of this anecdote shows her capacity to enjoy a joke at her own expense. I like best the story of her unappreciated teasing of Samuel Butler, told by Desmond MacCarthy in his Foreword to *Thackeray's Daughter*: 'I recall,' MacCarthy says, 'Samuel

Butler telling me that when he had told her he was at work on a
book about "The Sonnets," she had said to him, "O, Mr.
Butler, I hope you think they were written by Anne Hathaway
to Shakespeare?" As he repeated this to me, he looked gravely
over his spectacles and murmured, "Poor lady, poor lady, that
was a silly thing to say." He had forgotten that his last book had
been that fantastic feat of attribution, "The Authoress of the
Odyssey." ' MacCarthy goes on: 'The mildness of her comments
never diminished their point. Once when someone quoted, à
propos of some youthful attack on established reputations,
Ibsen's phrase about "the young generation knocking at the
door," Lady Ritchie remarked pensively, "But, alas, they never
knock." ' Virginia Woolf made use of both these repartees in
her characterization of her aunt as Mrs. Hilbery in *Night and
Day*.

Still another picture of Aunt Anny's humour and sentiment
simultaneously in action is furnished by Mary MacCarthy in a
delightful narrative of the expedition to Westminster Abbey,
to superintend the work of the sculptor, Mr. Onslow Ford,
while he gave William Makepeace Thackeray's bust a needed
trim of its side whiskers. 'Mrs. MacCarthy went with her on
"this odd little errand." They found the bust had been removed
from the Poets' Corner, and waiting for them in the crypt were
the Dean, Onslow Ford the sculptor looking very cross, and his
assistant. With her old lady's irresistible charm, Anny con-
strained Mr. Onslow Ford much against the grain to carry out
the work. Then she triumphantly followed the bust which,
with its now shortened whiskers, was replaced in its niche.
"Aunt Anny is a little emotional as she gets into the victoria." '

Whether Lady Ritchie's capacity to turn a striking phrase
is to be considered an aspect of her humour, it certainly forms
a notable part of the charm of her memoirs. She had an eye for
the picturesque and the bizarre. I do not know whether, for
example, she is the only transmitter of the following story about
Jeremy Bentham; it is inserted in her reminiscences prefacing
Alfred, Lord Tennyson and His Friends (1893), a collection of
Julia Cameron's photographs, and she gives it as one of 'picturesque' Mr. Cameron's stories: how, having dined with Jeremy
Bentham, he had been shown the glass eyes that Bentham
intended to have substituted for his own after death, since he had

willed his body to the College of Physicians 'to be embalmed'; Bentham carried them around in his waistcoat pocket, just in case. But it is not so much for such blatantly peculiar facts that she is noted, as for her ability to render in a distinctively phrased image the humour or the poetry of the commonplace. She describes her London schoolroom as 'that long, bare room, only ornamented by a few large maps and a flowing border of governesses'. She remembers, of her grandmother Mrs. Carmichael-Smyth, that she 'used to walk out in a red merino cloak trimmed with ermine, which gave her the air of a retired empress wearing out her robes'. When Charlotte Brontë comes to call, 'she enters in mittens, in silence, in seriousness'. (P. 61.) It would be easy to multiply instances of this kind of poetic wit. Virginia Woolf summed it up: 'To embrace oddities and produce a charming, laughing harmony from incongruities was her genius in life and in letters.'

The incongruities in Anny's life, and her successful struggle to embrace them, were sometimes evolved from her own delightful vagueness. 'The most ingrained Philistine could not remain bored, though bewildered [he] might be, by Miss Thackeray's charm. For it was a charm extremely difficult to analyze. She said things that no human being could possibly mean; yet she meant them. She lost trains, mixed names, confused numbers,' arrived at Down to visit Darwin a week ahead of time—which made him laugh at her in spite of the impropriety—but 'if she had gone on the right day poor Mr. Darwin would have been dying'. With all this scatter-brained impracticality, she was also penetratingly aware of the truth and worth of things around her. Her gaiety and love of life were irresistible and unquenchable.

Among Anne Thackeray Ritchie's close friends, one should number, of course, certain of her relatives besides her father and her sister and the Stephens. She was very close to her sisters-in-law, Emily Ritchie, Blanche Warre-Cornish, and Augusta Freshfield. With Mrs. Brookfield, her father's friend, she was on intimate terms, except for an unfortunate period of estrangement after the publication of Thackeray's letters to Mrs. Brookfield. This breach was healed, however, before Mrs. Brookfield's death in 1896. (Lady Ritchie's views on the subject of publishing private letters were mixed and unstable, but more

1   Mme de l'Etang

2   Mrs James Pattle
(née Adeline de l'Etang)

3 Mrs John Jack
(née Maria Pat

4 Old Little Holland House

5 Julia Jackson
(later Mrs Leslie Stephen)

6 Virginia Pattle
(later the Countess Somers)

7 Mrs Richard Strachey
(née Jane Maria Grant)

8 Jane Maria Grant, Lady Str

9 Lady Strachey in later life

10   Gen. Richard Strachey and Mrs Strachey, with the Hooker-Gray party
at La Veta Pass in Colorado, July 1877

11   The annual united march of Women's Suffrage groups in
London, 1908. Lady Strachey is in
the front of the procession

12 Anne Isabella Thackeray,
Lady Ritchie

13 Mrs Richmond Ritchie
(née Anne Isabella Thacke

Mary Warre-Cornish
MacCarthy

15 Mrs Desmond MacCarthy (née Mary
Warre-Cornish), playing croquet at
Newington House, the home of
Ethel Sands, in 1913

16 Molly MacCarthy, her daughter Rachel (Lady David Cecil),
and Ralph Partridge

17 The Memoir Club, in session about 1943

of that later.) The George M. Smiths, hers and her father's publisher and his charming wife Elizabeth and their daughters, were beloved friends and often in the early days after Thackeray's death very substantial benefactors. Relations with the Carlyles were intimate, particularly with Mrs. Carlyle. It is interesting to trace Anny's feelings towards Carlyle after his wife's death. The Thackerays had never taken sides in the partisan divisions between Mr. and Mrs. Carlyle. When Mrs. Carlyle's letters, with Carlyle's notes, were published in 1883, Anny read her friend Mrs. Oliphant's article on them and reported to Emily Ritchie, then in India: 'the only thing I don't agree with her about, is her estimate of Carlyle and his notes. She calls them "silly," to me it seems so inexpressibly affecting that he, the grumbling old cynic should have been so overpowered by love and remorse, that he takes the whole world into his confidence.' She feels that 'a 1000 people will be happier for knowing how unhappy those two "noble souls" were, and what Bogies they had to fight'. And to George M. Smith, of reading these same letters, she wrote that it 'does somehow make one forgive a great deal that made one angry. It is overwhelmingly interesting to me, and now I seem to know all the insides of the outsides, with which our childhood was passed, though at the same time I almost feel ashamed to know so much. Mrs. Carlyle was always our friend. I remember her telling me once, how nearly she had gone mad at one time—No wonder!' Anny is still defending Carlyle and these revelations at the height of the controversy over Froude's biography: 'The world has pointed its moral finger of late at the old man in his great old age, accusing himself in the face of all, and confessing the overpowering irritations which the suffering of a lifetime had laid upon him and upon her whom he loved. That caustic old man of deepest feeling, with an ill temper and a tender heart and a racking imagination, speaking from the grave, and bearing unto it that cross of passionate remorse which few among us dare to carry, seems to some of us now a figure nobler and truer, a teacher greater far, than in the days when his pain and love and remorse were still hidden from us all.'

But in 1902, she is coining the phrase about Carlyle (quoted by Virginia Woolf in 1924) in a letter to Reginald J. Smith: 'Old Carlyle was a god on one side of his face but a cross-grained,

ungrateful, self-absorbed old nut cracker on the other.' (*Letters*,
p. 260.) Two incidents in Anny's relations with Carlyle may
help to explain this mixed attitude. The first Anny records, in a
letter to Mrs. Baxter, that after her father's death she had met
Carlyle on his horse, 'and he suddenly began to cry. I shall
always love him in future, for I used to fancy he did not care
about Papa.' The second was the sad fiasco of the tactlessly
selected, unwanted clock, presented to Carlyle by a group of
ladies, of whom Anne Ritchie was the leading spirit, as an
eightieth birthday present.

Another glimpse into Lady Ritchie's feelings about the
publishing of private letters is contained in an unpublished
hastily penned note to George M. Smith, about 1877, which
probably concerns the final edition of Mrs. Gaskell's *Life of
Charlotte Brontë*: 'Have you been reading Macmillan, and Jane
Eyre it is oh! so interesting and all the part about "G——"
"whom she likes to see looking pleased" and all her mysterious
offers. I do think it is a gt. shame to publish all this and her
faithful friend ought to be ashamed of herself.' Lady Ritchie
herself had a shockingly bad time of it over the publication of
one of Fitzgerald's letters to her father, which contained his
crude jibe at Elizabeth Barrett Browning, that brought down
the widower Browning's implacable ire on Fitzgerald's head.
Feeling herself involved in this mess, as her dead father's
defender, as well as Fitzgerald's, Anny attempted to play the
role of peace-maker, but with little success. It was a miserable
experience, and must have left her in a quandary over the
delicate question of the sanctity of private letters.

The literary friends of Anny included, besides Mrs. Oliphant
(whom Anny was visiting at Windsor on the night of Minny's
death), John Ruskin (whom Stephen and Anny visited shortly
thereafter at Brantwood), and the novelists Rhoda Broughton
and Henry James; the Brownings; George Eliot (who is said
to have been encouraged by Anny's example to marry the
very much younger Mr. Cross, after George Lewes' death); and
Logan Pearsall Smith, her near neighbour in Chelsea. All that
Chelsea group of early associates with Bloomsbury—Smith and
his sister Alys Russell, the Desmond MacCarthys, and others—
were the Ritchies' familiar friends and neighbours. So were the
elder Stracheys and their circle, including leading scientists.

Hester Ritchie was sent to Mlle. Souvestre's school in Wimbledon along with the Strachey children. And so also were the Tennyson circle at Freshwater, of whom Anny might be considered a prominent member. All the Ritchies, apparently, were of the Tennyson 'culte'. Both there, and in London earlier through her father's acquaintance with them, Anny became intimate with the Pattle sisters and their families.

She gives a delightful picture of the Pattle ladies *en masse* in her essay prefaced to *Alfred, Lord Tennyson and His Friends*: 'At a time when a young lady's wildest aspirations did not reach beyond crinolines and frisettes, Mrs. Cameron and other members of her family . . . realised for themselves the artistic fitness of things, the natural affinity between use and beauty.' The sisters had a gift for designing their own clothes in a kind of mixture of 'Paris art and the draperies of Raphael'. Anny was struck by their disregard for public opinion—'their own family was large enough to contain all the elements of interest and criticism'. She adds as a footnote to her observations on the Pattle sisters' 'unconventional rules for life': 'One marked peculiarity . . . was their respect for their own time; our philistine domestic rule, by which, from earliest hour in the morning, the women of the house are expected to be at the receipt of custom, to live in public, to receive any casual stranger, any passing visitor, was utterly ignored by them. They were busy with their own affairs, and anything they undertook they followed up with absolute directness of purpose. . . . They were unconscious artists, divining beauty and living with it.' (Pp. 12–13.)

Anny indeed sympathized with such liberated sentiments. Her essay, 'Toilers and Spinsters', commenced in 1860 and completed in 1873, anticipates Virginia Woolf's *A Room of One's Own*. Anny records therein her own ideas on the new feminism and her struggle to accept her (then) status as an old maid. She is amusing and eloquent on the rich life open to spinsters: 'Does Mudie refuse their subscriptions? Are they prevented from taking in *The Times*, from going out to dinner, from matchmaking, visiting, gossiping, drinking tea, talking, and playing the piano? If a lady has had three husbands, could she do more? May not spinsters, as well as bachelors, give their opinion on every subject, no matter how ignorant they may be;

travel about anywhere, in any costume, however convenient; climb up craters, publish their experiences, tame horses, wear pork-pie hats, write articles in the *Saturday Review*? They have gone out to battle in top-boots, danced on the tight-rope, taken up the Italian cause, and harangued the multitudes. They have gone to prison for distributing tracts; they have ascended Mont Blanc, and come down again,' etc. etc. The catch is, does the spinster, or the married woman, have enough money?

The style of the preceding quotation suggests something of the literary gift for spontaneous rhapsody which Anne Thackeray Ritchie and Virginia Woolf shared, and which I believe is owing to no influence of the one on the other but only to their common poetic gift and perhaps their common femininity. Quentin Bell noted it, in his *Bloomsbury* (1968), wherein he quotes from a letter of Aunt Anny's, dated 'Blois, Yesterday', an illustrative passage of 'a volatile kind of thought which hardly reappears in English literature before the publication of *The Voyage Out*': ' "All the old women have got their white caps on, the east wind has made every weather-cock shine. I can't think how to tell you what a lovely old place it is, sunny-streaked up and down, stones flung into *now* from St. Louis's days, others rising into carved staircases and gabions and gargoyles. This isn't a description—I wish it were—it isn't white or crisp enough, or high enough. There are broad flights and flights of steps going right up into the air, with the Bishop at the top and the Cathedral Service, and then the wonderful old garden and terrace and castle, and the ghosts of Guise and Henry III looking on through a doorway, and Catherine de Medici in her sunny bedroom opening upon loggias, and old roofs and birds and gardens. It is much more educated and sumptuous than other old towns." ' (P. 39.) This, though a rough draft in a letter, resembles the kind of vaulting flight of fancy frequently characteristic of Mrs. Woolf's style.

Anne Thackeray Ritchie experimented sometimes in her fiction with the fanciful life of the mind, in a manner that might almost be taken to foreshadow Virginia Woolf's type of stream of consciousness. For example, in *Old Kensington* (1873), an autobiographical novel about the life of the Morgans (i.e. the Thackerays), who live in Old Street, Kensington (i.e. Young Street), and their friends the Prinseps, appropriately disguised, who live in Little Holland House, a brief scene (Chapter XIX, p. 151) records the 'inner life' of Dolly Vanborough at the saints' day service in the chapel: 'What am I?' Dolly wonders. 'This is what she is at that instant—so she thinks at least: Some whitewashed walls, a light through a big window; John Morgan's voice echoing in an odd melancholy way, and her own two hands lying on the cushion before her. Nothing more . . . a bird's shadow . . . the branch of a tree. . . .'

In her critical essay 'Jane Austen' (in *Toilers and Spinsters*) Anny, who was a Jane-ite, notes however that the virtues of Austen's novelistic art are not accessible to the modern novelist: 'The clearest eyes must see by the light of their own hour. . . . What we have lost in calm, in happiness, in tranquillity, we have gained in intensity. Our danger is now, not of expressing and feeling too little, but of expressing more than we feel.' Living in a fuller and wider world than Jane Austen's, Anny and her contemporaries seek for 'a phase, a mood of mind, a sympathy'; she notes how George Eliot dwells on the 'inner minds of her creations rather than . . . their outward expression. . . . What trains of thought go sweeping through our brains! Man seems a strange and ill-kept record of many and bewildering experiences.' (Pp. 51–2, and p. 55.)

In *Mrs. Dymond* (1885)—Lady Ritchie's best novel—she interrupts herself in a descriptive passage to observe: 'There is a feeling which comes home to most of us at one time or another; philosophers try to explain it, poets to write it down only, musicians can make it into music, it is like a horizon to the present—a sense of the suggestion of life beyond its actual dim and rough shapings. This feeling gives a meaning to old stones and fluttering rags, to the heaps and holes on the surface of the earth, to the sad and common things as well as to those which are brilliant and successful.' She groped for the intensity and the extra dimension that Mrs. Woolf was to achieve.

The above passages show Anny at her most thoughtful and her most jejune, with their cursive, impromptu phrasing and their descents into the commonplace. Apparently, she wrote as naturally as the bird sings, but unlike her more artistic successor, she did not rewrite, select, and perfect.

Nevertheless, *Mrs. Dymond* gives the reader the same conviction to be derived from *The Newcomes*: that the leading characters are real people, and they move in a real, crowded, totally characteristic Victorian world of Britain and France. Probably this similarity rests on the same foundation, that both novels are indeed transmutations of actuality.

Thus it is appropriate that when Mrs. Woolf undertook to pay her best tribute to Aunt Anny, she should do it in *Night and Day*, a book modelled more on Jane Austen and the nineteenth-century art of fiction than any of her other novels. This leisurely volume with its rich evocation of Edwardian London is still a delight to read. Lady Ritchie knew of it, and of her niece's portrait of her in the character of Mrs. Hilbery; her daughter Hester said she was 'slightly taken aback' by it. But Lady Ritchie was no longer living when the novel was published in the autumn of 1919; she had died that February; and so she could not enjoy the general approval of Mrs. Hilbery, including Lytton Strachey's remarks in his review of *Night and Day*: 'The more of Mrs. Hilbery the better! An old fool—a woolly-brained chatter-box? We laugh a delighted assent—and go on to remember that we are laughing at one to whom alone love and the everlasting woman-wisdom have given the power of putting things right for her bewildered and tortured girl.' Thus Strachey repaid, with some asperity but marked respect, the championing which Aunt Anny had given his *Eminent Victorians* the year before.

Night and Day is like a Jane Austen novel in many ways, besides its general theme, which concerns self-discovery and launching into lifetime directions. It uses the same narrative and dramatic techniques, and the same basic design of pairs arranged in parallelograms, as in *Pride and Prejudice*. Occasionally, even a scene appears to echo an Austen one. A century of social history may be read at a glance by comparing the marvellous confrontation scene between Mr. Hilbery and Denham, Rodney, Katharine, and Cassandra (pp. 501–5) with the famous recognition scene between Mr. Bennet and Elizabeth and Darcy. But it is the composition of the characters which concerns us here.

None of the characters can be defined as a true-to-life portrait of any individual person in Mrs. Woolf's acquaintance, not even Mrs. Hilbery, though all are mixtures (sometimes too conspicuously) of traits and personalities that she knew in her family and friends. Mrs. Hilbery starts off like Aunt Anny, writing the biographical introductions to the Centennial Edition of Thackeray's works, aided by Katharine (i.e. Hester— in real life by Emily Ritchie, too). The description of Mrs. Hilbery's face (Chapter I, p. 14), with its mixture of youth and age, perplexity and optimism, its trustfulness and generosity, and the 'large blue eyes, at once sagacious and innocent', recalls the beautiful portrait of Lady Ritchie by J. S. Sargent. So too, her personality, as developed in the early chapters of *Night and Day*—her rambling, impulsive ways, socially very astute while appearing to be absent-minded and fluttery, and her habits of work as a writer (Aunt Anny's manuscripts used to baffle prin- ters, being covered with titbits and additions literally pinned to the pages), and her attitudes and sympathies—all are photographically like Lady Ritchie's. But in some details Mrs. Hilbery resembles Lady Strachey more than Lady Ritchie: her devotion to Elizabethan poetry and drama (whereas Lady Ritchie favoured the eighteenth- and nineteenth-century writers); her vague entry into rooms; her near-sightedness; the fear even that she might have to lose one eye. At one point (p. 452), Mrs. Woolf uses an image describing the confrontation of Mrs. Hilbery with Ralph Denham similar to one she would use ten years later in summing up her own and Leonard Woolf's feelings towards the aged Lady Strachey: 'From the distance of her age and sex she seemed to be waving to him, hailing him as a ship sinking beneath the horizon might wave its flag of greeting to another setting out upon the same voyage.' More- over, there may be some of Julia Stephen in Mrs. Hilbery's composition, since the little lecture on love which she gives Katharine (pp. 511–12) resembles the conversation between Mrs. Ramsay and the girls, late at night in their bedroom, in *To the Lighthouse*. But all this recognition of ingredients in the fictional Mrs. Hilbery is merely to underline the Austen-like realism of *Night and Day*, for the selection and combination into a new unity of truly observed living models—of actions and scenes as well as of personalities—are the essence of the realistic novelist's art, which furnishes the granite underneath all Virginia Woolf's rainbows.

Virginia Woolf, strange to relate, considered Katharine Hilbery to be mainly a portrait of Vanessa Bell, to whom she dedicated this novel; but of course Hester Ritchie's position as the daughter of Aunt Anny is clearly there. More importantly, Katharine is a mask for Virginia Woolf herself. The experiences of all three young women in their relations to their parents and their friends are drawn upon. Ralph Denham is supposed to be a fairly close portrait (*mutatis mutandis*) of Leonard Woolf; and William Rodney is a figure composed of traits common to young upper-class intellectuals, graduates of the university, with whom Vanessa and Virginia Stephen were thrown during the efforts of their family to introduce them to society in Kensington. Mary Datchet resembles Janet Case, a Newnham graduate who was a great friend of Virginia Woolf and her tutor in Greek; but she also has some elements of Philippa Strachey, especially in her activities in the Women's Suffrage cause. Virginia Woolf herself, like Katharine, once worked for a while as a volunteer in the Russell Square office. The evening party at Mary Datchet's flat, when Rodney reads his paper, is more like a meeting of the Neo-Pagans, or Middleton Murry, Katherine Mansfield, Carrington, the Bagenals, etc., than it is like an Old Bloomsbury evening.

As for Mr. Hilbery, he is basically a portrait of Sir Richmond Ritchie, but with some admixture of Sir Leslie Stephen, and perhaps even of Sir Richard Strachey. Certain traits would identify him immediately as Ritchie to those who knew him in real life: the love of music and the little green stone fingered like worry beads; but his researches into minutiae of literary biography and his hearty advocacy of the novels of Sir Walter Scott are more reminiscent of Sir Leslie Stephen, though Sir Richmond Ritchie was also deeply engaged in literature. A word picture of Ritchie in a recent memoir shows the relation of the real-life character to the fictional Mr. Hilbery: 'He was a most formidable person—six foot three inches tall and heavily built, with a glance at once humorous, sardonic, and shattering, a rich voice, sober but expressive gestures, and sharp and mordant wit ready to flay the self-complacent and blast the sentimental. He was a past master in probing people's weaknesses—"For thirty years," he once said, "I have studied, with considerable success, the art of making people lose their tempers." '

The large family of Otways, the Hilberys' cousins, may be founded on the Stracheys (Marjorie Strachey was convinced that she was the model for Cassandra Otway, though alas, not in looks). But as we have seen, among these Anglo-Indian families, such clans of cousins were all over the map.

The fondly humorous amenity of Virginia Woolf's attitude towards her Aunt Anny and towards the past she represented, and her feeling for the continuity and the influence of that past, are fictionally embodied in the climax of the plot of *Night and Day*. Katharine Hilbery has suffered, as Virginia Woolf did, under the constriction of her parents' influence: 'The glorious past, in which men and women grew to unexampled size, intruded too much upon the present, and dwarfed it too consistently, to be altogether encouraging to one forced to make her experiment in living when the great age was dead.' (P. 33.) But at the climax of Katharine's dilemma, it is Mrs. Hilbery who plays the role of *dea ex machina*. Katharine and Denham have nothing impeding their happy union, at last, except the conventional kind of lovers' misunderstandings and missed rendezvous. Mrs. Hilbery has ascertained Katharine's state of mind towards Denham; she then goes, secretly, straight to Denham, finds out that he wants to marry Katharine, and sweeps him up in her exquisitely ridiculous carriage ride all round London on matter-of-course errands, winding up in Chelsea at the house in Cheyne Walk, where the happy reconciliation takes place. Thus the past makes the present and the future.

Perhaps Virginia Woolf agreed essentially with the idea in her aunt's conclusion to 'A Discourse on Modern Sybils', wherein Lady Ritchie, considering Rudyard Kipling's question, 'Why go on constantly dwelling on the past?', avers that she would have answered him thus: 'Because . . . the past holds us in its noble grip and it *is* the present.' The sense of the past as 'the eternal moment' is implicit in Mrs. Woolf's other tribute to Aunt Anny, her review of Lady Ritchie's published *Letters*, which is largely a character sketch. The review begins and ends with Lady Ritchie's earliest memory of herself as a two-year-old dancing in the street to the music of the street-organ near Russell Square. Mrs. Woolf concludes: 'the music to which she dances, frail and fantastic, but true and distinct, will sound on outside our formidable residences when all the brass bands of literature have (let us hope) blared themselves to perdition.'

6

Mary Josefa MacCarthy, née Warre-Cornish
(1882–1953)

IT IS fitting to conclude this book of backgrounds with a chapter on Lady MacCarthy, author and appreciator of memoirs, and founder of the Memoir Club, that inner circle of the Bloomsbury Group which might be described as its heart. But there is also a degree of illogic in placing her with the older ladies already discussed, or in suggesting that she was only in the background of the Bloomsbury Group. She belonged to the same generation as Virginia Woolf, outliving her by twelve years. From about 1910 onwards, even more than her husband, Desmond MacCarthy, she was very much a part of the Group. But at the same time she was distinct from it; she differed with their agnosticism and pacifism, and she was much more conservative than they towards political and social questions and ethical customs. She was the one, however, who from her Chelsea home in Wellington Square first gave them the affectionate nickname 'the Bloomsberries'.

In an appreciation of Lady MacCarthy, written some years after her death, Sir William Haley described her as 'a quizzically gay, shrewd, and totally charming woman. . . . There was always a nice, delicate turning-point in her friendship when she became Molly. . . .' I shall take the liberty of calling her Molly in this sketch of her life, personality, and career, for I intend to put it sometimes in her own words with the feeling of intimate acquaintance that they convey.

To get to know Molly, one should begin by reading *A Nineteenth-Century Childhood* (1924), wherein she introduces us to herself and her family under the pseudonym of Kestell (an ancestral Devonshire name). Twenty years after the publication of that book, Molly began a sequel to it which she worked at intermittently and tried to complete during her last year of life. It remains an unfinished set of chapters and notes. Evidently she intended it to cover the quarter century from the death of Queen Victoria to the early 1920's, with one striking introductory chapter, entitled 'Dire Februaries', about the Second World War, as the vantage point from which it would be read. The book was to be titled 'The Bird Is On the Wing', a quotation from Omar Khayyam which she chose as expressing the sense of urgency to accomplish something vital while life remains; she noted that that was not Omar's cynically apathetic meaning, but she recognized the phrase as descriptive of her own personality.

Musing on Omar's words in her garden at Hampton by the Thames in 1952, she saw her seventy years as incredibly stretched out over the peace and security of her childhood and early married life in the late Victorian and Edwardian eras, through the horrors of the two world wars, and into the age of modern industrialism and technology. At the bottom of her mind was always the sense of her rootedness in the past, as one finds it expressed in her novel *A Pier and A Band* (1918); but her life growing out of that depth, she felt, had been racked and tormented by the explosions and distortions of the twentieth century.

She had long recognized herself as an habitual worrier, her anxieties running the gamut from trivialities of house-keeping through illnesses to international disasters. The basis of her tendency to worry seems to have been her deep devotion to order. 'In art, order is best,' she concludes a letter. Her own gifts did not include easy control of practicalities, and the disorders of the twentieth century around her made her nostalgic for the secure past. Self-discipline, a sharp and humorous sense of proportion, and, most of all, true courage were the correctives in her nature which prevented her from falling into self-pity or sentimentality.

These dreads represent the deepest notes of sadness and suffering, a kind of diapason beneath a very complex, quick, imaginative, humorous personality. Those who knew her well testify to her capacity to live fully in the present; her fresh-ness of spirit and sympathetic responsiveness, her inventive mind and witty conversation made her an engaging com-panion.

A few facts may be added to interpret *A Nineteenth-Century*

Childhood and give Molly her proper historical setting. Her father, Dr. Francis (Frank) Warre-Cornish, was master of Holland House at Eton College when Molly was born. He came from a family of distinguished gentleman farmers and clergy-men in south Devonshire, described by his cousin Vaughan Cornish in a book dedicated to him, *Kestell, Clapp, and Cornish* (1947). He had met and married Blanche Ritchie, a cousin of W. M. Thackeray, when she was only eighteen, at her widowed mother's home in Ottery St. Mary. A book might be written about Blanche Warre-Cornish; indeed there is reputed to be a collection in print of her 'entirely unpredictable' sayings on social occasions, which is perhaps the anthology compiled by Logan Pearsall Smith, as a joke, in 1935, and never circulated. The Misses Strachey told me one such (perhaps apocryphal) remark made by Mrs. Warre-Cornish to a sixteen-year-old Eton boy sitting beside her at a musicale, when some particularly excruciating music was being played: 'Doesn't it remind you of the pangs of childbirth?'

Both the Warre-Cornishes were highly musical and literary. Their children were surrounded with music and literature in that cultivated household. In the order of their birth, the children were Margaret (Mag), Dorothy (Dodo), Francis Thackeray, Hubert (Bert), Gerald (Jerry), Charlotte (Char, or Charty), Mary (Moll—Francis refers to her once in a letter as 'Saint Moll'), and Cecilia. Margaret and Dorothy remained unmarried; Margaret was the intellectual one, helping to tutor the younger children and teaching for a while at Northlands School; Dorothy was frail, retiring, and devoted to good works, but surprisingly, could manage unruly ponies. Francis died young of illness in India in 1901, after a ten-year career in the Bengal Lancers; he was an artist and fond of the outdoors, tremendously keen on hunting and racing. Hubert and Gerald proceeded from Eton to Cambridge. Gerald entered the Church, but was too left-wing for an ordinary clerical career; he was killed tragically in the Battle of the Somme in 1916; a book of his stories was edited and published by his good Cambridge friend and brother-in-law Desmond MacCarthy, a year later. Charlotte married Reginald Balfour, a classical scholar, who was briefly in the army during the Boer War. Cecilia's husband, Admiral W. W. Fisher, was the brother of the historian, H. A. L. Fisher, whom we have encountered among the Pattle sisters' in-laws.

Molly was born on August 14, 1882, probably at the Warre-Cornishes' country home, 'The Chough's Nest', near Lynton in north Devon. The family, accompanied by servants and mountains of baggage, went there for the Easter and the summer holidays regularly every year until near the end of the century. That beautiful wild countryside, Exmoor and the coast of the Bristol Channel, forms the principal setting of *A Pier and A Band*. Much of that novel's scenery and its heroine's relation to the outdoors and to the neighbours in the story must incorporate Molly's own youthful recollections. But most of her childhood and youth was spent at Eton; from the summer of 1893 on, the Warre-Cornishes occupied 'The Cloisters', the residence of the Vice-Provost.

Molly was educated in the schoolroom at home by governesses and by her sister Mag. Her father had charge of the Eton College library, which could be entered by a door directly from the Vice-Provost's house; his speciality in developing that library's collection, so Vaughan Cornish tells us, was 'early books of the Aldine Press'. He also published a number of his own works on English social and ecclesiastical history, the *History of Chivalry* (1901) being one of the best, and he contributed the volume on Jane Austen to the English Men of Letters series. In addition there are three books of his fiction: a long leisurely Trollopian novel *Sunningwell* (1899), with its sequel *Dr. Ashford and His Neighbours* (1914), and a further collection of five novelettes, *Darwell Stories* (1910). Blanche Warre-Cornish also published two novels, *Alcestis* (2 vols., 1873), a historical novel about opera in Dresden, and *Northam Cloisters* (2 vols., 1882); but her most agreeable book is *Some Family Letters of W. M. Thackeray, together with Recollections by His Kinswoman* (1911), containing an enchanting child's-eye view of Thackeray as a visitor to her grandmother's home in Paris. Voluminous reading and writing, especially letter-writing in that close-knit family with its ramified clans of relatives, were as natural as breathing. Molly's learning came chiefly from her lifelong association with books and writers.

One literary visitor to the Warre-Cornish home was Maurice Baring. He liked to play, and they were literary enough themselves to play with him, a very intellectual game he invented called the Style Game. Each player had to write a piece of prose or verse on some incongruous subject, in the style of some great writer assigned to him. For example, the difficulties of a family attempting to meet each other at a railway station, in the style of Jane Austen or of Laurence Sterne. Baring, apparently, was the judge of the contest. Incidentally, he remained a lifelong friend of Molly and Desmond MacCarthy, and perhaps occasionally a literary adviser to Molly, who submitted her plans for the unfinished memoirs to him for suggestions (which she did not follow). But Desmond, who was an excellent coach of writing, was naturally her principal critic.

I wish I knew the full inwardness of a tale about Maurice Baring and Molly, when he is said to have done her up in a large brown paper parcel which he was to try to smuggle onto a train.

From the Anglican convent school near Eton where Molly spent a year, as she describes in *A Nineteenth-Century Childhood*, she proceeded to Northlands, a school for girls run by a Miss Weisse, who had as protégé the distinguished musicologist Professor Donald Tovey. Her education there was given a solid grounding in the liberal arts, including French and German; but for all her aptitude for language, she was not an expert speaker in later life of these foreign tongues. She had a few months' residence in France in her latter teens to perfect her French, probably in 1900–1, and stayed on for a year in Germany, 1901–2. These foreign residences were to serve as finishing her education. She reports fully and very interestingly on the German experience both in the heroine Perdita Villiers' adventures in *A Pier and A Band* and in 'A German Court Before the War', one of the memoirs included in her volume *The Festival* (1937). She is said to have received a proposal of marriage from a German officer in the army, possibly named Pauker, as she notes in her topical outlines for the unfinished memoirs. Whether or not she met 'Fitzgerald' (her fictional name for Desmond MacCarthy) again in Germany, as Perdita Villiers does, at any rate she came home unengaged to live again at the Cloisters with frequent social excursions as a debutante to London.

Desmond MacCarthy, born in Plymouth in 1877 into a banking family of Irish extraction, was about the same age as Molly's brothers Hubert and Gerald, whom he undoubtedly knew at Eton and at Trinity College, Cambridge (1894–7). It was through that friendship that he became acquainted with the Warre-Cornish family and took to squiring around the younger daughters during the London season, as he began his long, distinguished career as journalist, critic, and editor. The dance at the amusingly named Mrs. Tallboys' (in contrast to 'Lady A's. She only knows about twelve young men—all under life-size or with squints.'—*A Nineteenth-Century Childhood*, p. 84) is probably a realistic glimpse of the social life that succeeded to the Little Holland House society in the days of the Prinseps. The young Warre-Cornishes could have met Vanessa and Virginia Stephen (not to mention also the younger Stracheys) at such balls, or at their aunt Mrs. Freshfield's home in Chelsea. But there is no evidence that Desmond and Molly MacCarthy knew these later lifelong friends until after their marriage.

Molly tells the story of her engagement to Desmond, in 1904, in a paper entitled 'Nervous Breakdown 30 Years Ago. An Account', which she read to the Memoir Club about 1934, and which she meant to serve as the fourth chapter of 'The Bird Is On the Wing'. It narrates a long, nightmarish illness that settled on her inexplicably about six weeks after her engage-ment, and that involved a period of supposed recuperation in a London nursing home and at the seaside; the whole dismal experience was complicated by the fact that her nurse turned out to be a drug addict, which Molly did not discover until the nurse attempted to dose her with some of her own 'medicine'. Molly escaped, while the woman was under the influence, and tele-graphed her mother. The next day Mrs. Warre-Cornish and Desmond both came to the rescue, and Mr. Oscar Browning, who stayed outside in the garden. 'He is waiting there for us,' her mother explained, 'as we will dine with him when you settle for the night, darling, and that will be so cheerful for Desmond!' Blessed normality was restored.

After their 'happy and baking hot August country wedding', July 10, 1906 (Molly's memory for dates was unreliable), Desmond took Molly, on their honeymoon, for the first of their visits to Thomas Hardy in Dorchester. Her description of 'A Visit to Thomas Hardy'—which she clipped to her unfinished chapter 3—is contained in a fragment of manuscript, apparently a speech on poets she had known, which she may have given to some circle of ladies at Oare, Wiltshire, in the 1920's. The fragment begins with nostalgic recollections of Tennyson's verse and probably of the poet laureate himself, whom she had known when, as a child, she visited at the Porch in Farringford: ' . . . I will not keep you singing "Tirra lirra by the river" with the Lady of Shalott, or quote Morte d'Arthur and pass a few seconds with the romantic legendary knights I so loved. "So all day long the noise of battle rolled among the mountains by the winter sea—" began the tale of death. Oh! to think of it, that at that time in the '90's great wars seemed to be confined to old history books and ballads; tyrants, murderers dungeons daggers rebellions and bloody exterminations were never to come into our safe life again! All just shut up in history books—' With a great leap she comes to 'a very different old poet', Thomas Hardy. Desmond 'had known Hardy for some years and they had plenty to say to one another'. Hardy, just finishing the *Dynasts*, his wife, the MacCarthys, and a clergyman, Mr. Perkins, a bicycling companion of Hardy's, lunched together at Hardy's house. Mrs. Hardy, with whom Molly had chiefly to converse, struck her as a bitter, complaining old woman, who though she was still proud of being the heroine of *A Pair of Blue Eyes*, had forgotten all tenderness towards her husband. She quite shocked Molly with her complaints of Hardy's ingratitude —you would have thought that she had written his novels herself; but after her death in 1912, Molly remarked, Hardy remembered only the early happy years of that marriage. Molly described Hardy's talk as vigorous and though gloomy never whining. He told the story of remembering his grandmother ironing in the heat of summer and recalling the similar day of Marie Antoinette's execution. He saw the MacCarthys to the gate as they left, and she remembered him walking back into the house past the wet bushes, to work again at his melancholy *Dynasts*.

In the autumn, Desmond and Molly settled into the living-rooms of a farmhouse in Suffolk, the Green Farm, at Ampton, just north of Bury St. Edmunds. The rent of this dwelling was part of Desmond's pay for his new job as editor of *The New Quarterly*. It stood on the estate of Arthur Paley, the very wealthy and eccentric descendant of old Archbishop Paley, author of *Evidences of Christianity*. Desmond had known Arthur Paley through school, Eton, and Trinity College, and 'understood the failings of this strange being'; it was the one friendship Paley 'kept and valued' throughout his short life. Molly found him hopeless: ' "Desmond, I shall myself never be able to get on with Arthur," I said, rather disappointed, after a few months of attempts had failed. "Well, don't try. You'll get used to one another." ' She felt herself 'lacking in Desmond's very special gift for getting on with people who seemed to almost everybody round us to be difficult'. But there were plenty of more agreeable connections brought to the farmhouse study by the magazine business, the 'varied writers' who were contributors, some not yet famous, but soon to be so: 'G. E. Moore . . . G. Lowes Dickinson; Chesterton; Granville Barker; Lytton Strachey; Maurice Baring; George Trevelyan . . .'

Molly describes this upstairs book-lined study, where she read aloud to 'Des', enjoying the fire (coal or logs), the candles, the green-shaded lamp, his pipe, two spaniels, the bare board floor with fur hearth-rug, the windows overlooking the cow-sheds and the milking, the village green and the row of cottages beyond. 'Desmond had an entirely individual peculiarity when pleased and happy and in need of expressing this, of quite suddenly giving a long rub to his eyes with both hands, rather like a fly that seems to be vigorously washing its face. This curious spontaneous and unique gesture always meant that he was rapturously contented; and at the same moment he would exclaim out loud, "My happiness is more than I can bear," which exaggeration made us both burst out laughing, and contentedly enjoy the moment.'

'Each morning, all the winter, ice lay on our water jugs on rising. . . .' She did not mind it then, being 'young and vital', as she later came to mind the cold seriously. She read aloud to Desmond passages from Shakespeare and Keats describing winter. While Desmond worked, she went about the village gradually making friends with the simple folk who lived in the red-brick, slate-roofed cottages, or she drove a governess cart, drawn by a 'café-au-lait coloured pony with his white mane, found for us by the farm bailiff', on errands and rambles, some-times to the workhouse of Bury St. Edmunds, 'with a basket of

apples and a basket of spectacles', or books to lend, or a favourite
present of 'Housekeeper's Cake'. Sometimes she read aloud to
Lizzie Clark, while Lizzie ironed—Hardy's *Under the Greenwood
Tree* and Stevenson's *Treasure Island*. Lizzie took 'Drink and the
Devil had done for the rest' very seriously; she knew; but she
enjoyed the style—'Go on, Ma'am, please.' Once a child
disconcerted Molly with the Suffolk aptitude to take a dim view
of the future; the child, to whom she had given a doll as a prize,
'after nice thanks' added, 'That will be something to remember
you by when you're dead, Ma'am.' Since Molly 'had scarcely
reached' her 'twenty-fifth year at the time, the reminder seemed
a little startlingly direct'. Sometimes she helped the chemist
dispense the medicines that he was to give away to the poor of
the village and charge to Paley's account—a typical generosity
of Paley, for all his curmudgeonly behaviour.

Once Molly and Desmond accompanied Paley to the Assizes
in Ipswich, her first visit to a court of law. As she recalls the
cases heard, a petty highway robbery, 'cases of drunks, cases of
theft by poaching', she contrasts these simple crimes with those
of modern times. Finally, 'A low case of murder;—a woman's
murder of her own child.' Molly reconstructs it imaginatively
in all its horror—the drowning, the lace collar floating, the
woman's apathy and sheepish smile when the judge held the
collar to his own neck to see if she recognized it.

On her solitary rambles through the country in the governess
cart, Molly indulged her interest in the past with visions of
'Suffolk ghosts'—the eloping Lady Sarah Bunbury, who
eventually became Lady Napier, mother of famous soldiers and
sailors; or Oliver Goldsmith on his way to visit the Henry
Bunburys at Barton, for the New Year—poor Oliver, so soon to
die! How much Molly appreciated the eighteenth-century way
of life! 'Horses and carriages alone had carried them about;
(how impossible it had been to greatly hurry!) The Victorians
then had next hurried up by steam, in trains . . .' but now in
Suffolk she was in the late Edwardian period. Speeding motors,
chromium and nickel plate, Mass Production, Universal Indus-
trialization and the mechanization of warfare—these devasta-
tions were on their way. But at the time the Edwardian era
seemed frivolous: 'the fashionable round of Ascot, Goodwood,
Cowes, great Austrian winter "sports" and house parties and

back to the London season and more house parties and Scotch grouse moors, for ever! Awfully jolly no doubt!' Molly recalls the long tailored suits fashionable for women in that day—'dowdy to a later generation'—and the habit of recording house parties in group photographs. Then the photographer 'pushed off the cap of the lens—and there they all were! Stiffly fixed! and now pasted into the large heavy old photograph books that we have inherited from the eighties and nineties, how amusing they are to look over, and behold the youth of handsome men and women, that could be to us only *old*, passed away.'

A few snapshots of Molly, and a great many of Desmond MacCarthy, remain in the marvellous albums left by Lady Ottoline Morrell. Molly is to be seen in the gardens at Garsington or at Broughton Grange (this would be in the second and third decades of this century), usually playing croquet. She wears a long dark skirt and a light blouse, and her face is always shaded by a broad beribboned hat. She was not a pretty woman; her plain but attractive features were marked by huge round dark brown eyes, round cheeks and chin, and a rather too wide mouth that dropped markedly at the left corner, like 'an ironic hyphen', as one friend described it. She was of medium size with a graceful figure, rather bosomy, and she moved slowly in later life owing to rheumatism. Two portraits are known to exist, one a miniature of her at about age three—a solemn cherub with blonde dutch-cut hair—and the other in middle age, painted by Neville Lytton, the grandson of the novelist and son of Lord Robert Lytton, Lady Strachey's much admired friend. Molly's speaking voice was normally unpretentious, but she was capable (with her skill for mimicry) of imitating the so-called Bloomsbury voice, with a satiric emphasis, underlining words unexpectedly (as she underlined them habitually in letters) and with so much wit and originality that one had to listen to her. She dearly loved the ridiculous and would laugh till the tears flowed. But she was apparently camera-shy; in group photographs she is always in the background or to one side.

As variety to the contented country life in Suffolk, Molly sometimes accompanied Desmond to London. They would stay with his mother, 'Isachen'—'Chen' for short—she was German by birth and of French Huguenot ancestry—in her house in Chelsea. Or they would visit friends, not always literary friends, among others the Tatton Bowers, a wealthy family who were business friends of Desmond's father and whose great house in Prince's Gate stood out in Molly's recollection as the height of luxury. They enjoyed the theatre, especially Granville Barker's productions at the Court Theatre. They became acquainted with Max Beerbohm, and G. B. Shaw; they shared the enthusiasm for Ibsen's plays. They were involved to some extent in the Suffragette movement; every woman who knew Pippa Strachey was involved in promoting or taking part in the great Mud March. They visited the Sidney Webbs. But Desmond was against joining the Fabian Society. In one of her outlines for the unfinished memoirs, Molly explains: 'We were liberals—but not socialists. England for me was cut up into classes—that were not unnatural as the socialists avowed—we were like the flowers in the border arranged by botany. . . .'

In connection with 'Suffolk of my own' in her outlines, Molly proceeds to 'Gracie James and Livermere Rectory' and thence to Dick Sheppard, the outstanding vicar of St. Martin-in-the-Fields in later times. Livermere was the Suffolk parish church, apparently, which Molly may have attended. Now in London, the MacCarthys also met Belloc, who became a very close friend. Molly planned to discuss 'Religion here' in the memoirs. Though not describable as a devout Christian, she remained always a believer and took the part of established religion in arguments with her agnostic friends. As one of them described her position, she would 'more or less agree to dismiss religion for the educated, but would say "Yes, yes, but the working classes *must* have it," with an impatient and comically reproving frown'. Another testified that 'she really believed that we should be happier had the Reformation never happened and all had gone on as rather lapsed Catholics like the French'. Towards the end of her life, she returned to the Church.

Before the MacCarthys moved from Green Farm to the house in Wellington Square, Chelsea, which they purchased in 1910, they made one extraordinary trip of three months to South Africa, 'a curious experience', the nature of which we can only guess from Molly's jottings: 'Farm—baboons—Crew—Boers—loss of suitcase of lectures—Kruger's house—Jameson Raid—prison—Madhouse—Garden party atmosphere—but always

some fun going—Lionel Philips millionaire.' That 'loss of suitcase of lectures' would strike their acquaintances as a natural
event on any MacCarthy safari; objects in MacCarthy hands
were meant to be strewn in their wake.

In the summer of 1910, Molly accompanied Desmond to
Paris, when he went with Roger Fry on the important errand to
arrange the First Post-Impressionist Exhibition in London in
November of that year. She paid a visit to Picasso then; and
then or on later similar visits she met Gertrude Stein and Matisse
and Ambroise Vollard.

Desmond and Molly were blessed with three children, two
born during the Suffolk residence—Michael and Rachel—and
one in London, Dermod. They came along at two-year intervals between 1907 and 1911, and one wonders how the young
couple managed, considering all their manifold activities.
Molly's notes for the memoirs always carefully append to the
mention of the children's births, or to the housekeeping in
London: 'Unquestionable that one had a nanny'—'Nannies still
an institution'. The house in London was 'All so easy because
of servant era still going'. That made possible going out in
the evenings. Not just to the theatre, but to 'Fancy Dress parties'
and charades (a favourite with Bloomsbury), for which Molly
wrote scripts, and 'evenings with Duncan and Ottoline', and
'preoccupying flirtations'—'Clive Bell, and going about'—and
'Getting to know Vanessa and Virginia'; and Ballet; and 'Henry
James and the evening with Violet Bonham Carter after the
sinking of the Titanic'.

But Molly also records: 'A great deal of darning holes, and
cooking failures, and endless worrying bills . . . first efforts at
writing—early rising—London life and telephone distracting'.
The cares of managing the household weighed on her with
increasing heaviness through the First World War, as we shall
see, and with never enough money to go round. But on the other
hand, the children were delightful—an endless source of great
satisfaction, with only occasional worry, to their parents.

The four years between the MacCarthys' move to London
and the beginning of the First World War must have been on
the whole uncommonly gay and crowded with social life. Some
of this gaiety they shared and some of the time they went
their own ways, being both much in demand. There were the

'Bloomsbury evenings'; there was 'Ottoline and fantastical Bedford Square'; 'Newington and Howard Sturgis and Yeats'; 'Prince's Grill Room and Max'; and Soho and the Café Royal; and old Gunter's—'narrow shop—dark mahogany fittings—my meetings there with Charlotte—treat ices for young creatures with their fathers.' There were Arthur and Maggie Ponsonby and Dick Sheppard and St. James's Palace; Roger Fry and his studio and the Omega Shop, and a visit to Freshwater, with him along—a revival of Farringford, staying at the Porch with the children, the sea and meadows as ever, and the ghost of Mrs. Cameron. But we are spilling over into the war years, when the children had to be taken to the country to get away from the bombing. Added to the sorrows and hardships of the war were the deaths of Molly's father and mother and brother Gerald. Life was progressively grimmer.

It had reached a low ebb at Wellington Square as Christmas approached just after the 1918 armistice, when to Molly's delight an invitation came from Lady Ottoline for the whole family to spend the holidays at Garsington. What a prospect!— 'O ye fires, ye great Elizabethan beds, ye sofas and cushions, your books and lovely decorations! But oh ye hands and feet of scrimmaging little children!' Molly exclaimed in her rapturous letter of acceptance, in the vein of medieval Yuletide and fairy tale, winding up with Red Riding Hood's basket bearing their rations—'the vital butter!'

Molly wrote the story of this Christmas for her memoirs, marking it 'to be revised', which however, even in rough draft, gives a charming and revealing picture of her home life. 'Our household', she begins on the morning of Christmas Eve, 'was in a parlous state of confusion just now, for our nurse, its mainstay and comfort for eight years, had left us at last and alas! to marry,' and the Belgian cook had also been called home for holiday with her husband, a 'Sapeur'. 'Comfortable charwomen' were not to be had, with Christmas, influenza, and the wartime labour shortage. Only a little nursery maid from the country, Lavinia, was present to aid, chiefly as 'a fourth at ping-pong in the Nursery'.

'The running up and down of four flights of the tall old London house and the incessant cooking and getting together of meals . . . and getting the fires lit in the old grates . . . and beds made and clothes from the laundry unpacked, and putting the children to bed and getting Michael off to school in time, having had his breakfast, and taking the children out, to mention some of countless details, had all been very exhausting. . . .'

About noon this Christmas Eve, Rachel was gaitered, Molly fur-coated, Michael was 'sliding the suitcases down the stairs; finally Desmond had put the last words to a review of a new edition of Walter Savage Landor's books, and having packed his great bag of books, had now dashed out to cash a cheque and and get a taxi'. But then poor Dermod upstairs was audibly sick in the bathroom. Brought down to the dining-room sofa, he had his temperature taken—influenza—everybody else must go quickly and catch the train, while Molly stayed behind with Dermod. Protests, sorrow, sobs, but 'in another moment they had banged the door of the cab and ticked away, leaving a sudden hush in the hall'. From the dining-room came the sound of Dermod sobbing; upstairs, he soon cheered up and went to sleep. Then Molly realized that 'there was no food left in the house, and the shops would be shut in a few hours' time'. She got on the phone to secure some friend or relative to come and stay while she marketed, but nobody was at home. 'My sister Margaret was nursing in France, the others were all far away, so was Desmond's mother. . . . There was nothing in it but to leave the child alone with his fever and go out and collect remedies and food.' Which she did, through all the crowds and the beginning of a snowstorm. When she returned to the nursery Dermod was peacefully asleep, and she too retired for a nap.

'Either "Martha" or "Mary",' she continued, 'takes control of most young married women when they rest, and as far as I myself was concerned sometimes with "Mary" I would have the good fortune to die quickly away into a delicious day dream . . . but far oftener it was "Martha" who laid herself down at one's side and her expanse of bed then became "the grumbolian plain." She had been with me on this occasion since earliest morning and I was heartily sick of her and would have been thankful to get rid of her, but here sure enough she was, waiting for me; reminding me of . . . air raids, influenza, servant troubles. . . .' Molly continues 'Martha's' grumbling in a dialogue form, touching on the handicap of women not having

'really strong muscles', the bad weather, the crowded streets—
'God seemed quite suddenly to have created two or three million
people more for London, all middle aged and all ugly.' 'I
laughed at that idea and the bed shook a little with my mirth
. . . and the glowing coals in the fireplace fell in and broke apart
at the moment sending heartening flames up the chimney, and
gentle light and shadows about the walls of the darkened
nursery inviting peace. But Martha never had a grain of
humour, and also she was not in the least susceptible to the
poetry of the fire; and she had not done yet. "Nearly everything
in the house is broken," she whined on. "I know it's thought
very wrong to take up a workman's time for a moment now,
but how long can one go on with broken springs and cracked
crockery, and curtains hanging in shreds? and the paint
knocked off everything? and one puts one's toes through the
sheets every night, and pyjamas and nightgowns tear at a touch,
and everything perpetually needs mending." After all, Virginia
Woolf who rather approves of rags and tatters last time she came
to the house, said, "Oh, you *must* have some repairs done—the
entrails of your chairs are all over the floor." '

'Dermod's temperature was normal by Boxing Day and we
had got through the time fairly well making toast and hot red
currant tea and other salubrious beverages with the help of
the steaming nursery kettle, and with painting and reading
aloud. . . ."The King of the Golden River" by Ruskin was the
book we were reading.'

Molly's appreciation and understanding of young children
come out clearly in the whole story.

At some time earlier in 1918, Molly had started the Novel
Club, with the inner circle of the Bloomsbury Group, in order
to *make* Desmond write his novel—he never did. The Novel
Club was a revival of the notion of a literary circle among these
friends such as the play-reading club of ten years earlier. This
one lasted the year, but then Molly revised it into the Memoir
Club, which began meeting in the winter of 1919–20 and persisted until the mid-1960's. Molly's note card of invitation reads
as follows:

'*The Memoir Club* will have its opening meeting on Friday, the
27th inst. [probably February 1920] at 9 o'CLOCK PRECISELY at

25 Wellington Square. It is expected that a few opening papers
will be shown up by everyone—showing that people have
thought out their probable manner of managing their memoirs,
and after that a chapter once a month is hoped for!

'Probable members of the Memoir Club; Roger Fry—Desmond
—Maynard—Duncan—Proby—Virginia—Sidney Waterlow—
Clive Bell—Vanessa—and etc.

'The first meeting will open with a short discussion.

'Mary MacCarthy, Secretary and drudge of the Club.'

Molly remained in this role of convener and 'drudge' for
many years, until, at the meeting of January 23, 1946, she made
what is reported to have been an excruciatingly funny farewell
speech—no record of which, alas, remains—and the leadership
passed in turn briefly to Vanessa and Quentin Bell, and eventually to Frances Partridge.

Molly's leadership in forming the Memoir Club was in no
sense authoritarian, and the group carried on almost from the
first under its own momentum, since evidently it really met
a felt need of its members. Leonard Woolf described it in a letter
to me of June 22, 1961, as 'Simply a form of amusement. We
confined it to intimate friends, and it was decided that we should
write memoirs and read them aloud in rotation. That in fact
is what has happened since, though some have died and new
members have joined.' Others thought of it as an opportunity
to share unfinished manuscripts or unpublishable ones. It is
obvious that a large number of these first drafts found their way
into the members' published memoirs and collections of essays.
Virginia Woolf's contributions, however, must not have been
published (Mr. Woolf assured me that none are in her collected
essays), except perhaps for a few passages in her biography of
Roger Fry. I suspect that she would read aloud from her diary
or working notebooks, when it was her turn to perform. Her
1919 diary begins in January with the idea that she will let it
form the basis of her memoirs, which she looks forward to
writing. A three-page fragment, however, of a Memoir Club
paper of hers is to be found in the Berg Collection of the New
York Public Library; it concerns Maynard Keynes and Desmond
MacCarthy; an annotation explains that Molly had asked her
to contribute, though Virginia felt that other members were

better qualified, but how could she refuse Molly anything?—
'she is so charming'.

It must have taken considerable tact on Molly's part to
arrange the Club meetings and bring them to pass. She was ably
assisted by Maynard and Lydia Keynes, at whose home in
Gordon Square the dinner-party, followed by the readings,
frequently took place. There were no elected officers and no one
presided at the meetings. The Club had only two unbreakable
rules: No one should ever take offence at anything, and no new
member could be introduced into the Club except by the unani-
mous vote of all current members, conducted by secret ballot.
Molly herself broke that second rule once in inviting Jane Bussy
to join the Club (in January 1946) with only 'Charleston's vote
for her—we want another lady—she is ever so nice, and intelli-
gent. . . . I realize however I ought to have put her to the vote
and have behaved in a manner not right for Clubs— Put it down
to the war, please; *irregularities, haste,* the note that must now be
abandoned in the New Year. I get completely baffled over
the dates of our meetings! and the meetings are too few and far
between.' Keynes replied that he approved her 'high-handed
action in the matter of Janie. . . . I don't believe the Memoir
Club is capable of democratic procedure, and in that context
at least I approve of the Führer prinzip.' Molly sometimes took
the line that the Club should come to an end; writing to Keynes
about arrangements for the July 4, 1928, meeting, she thinks
that 'the Memoir Club will not ever meet again—but I think
the hour for the "Vale" has just arrived—and if Virginia reads
to us—and should it be a fine and sultry night, I think it will
be extraordinarily agreeable to meet all again for the last time,
for our readings'. But the Club continued and Molly endured
and tried to minimize the 'botherations', and after her retirement speech looked forward to 'the great honour of keeping the
Presidency without its anxieties'. To reduce bother and especially during the Second World War with the hazards of air raids,
the Club would read first, perhaps at Vanessa and Duncan's
studio in Bloomsbury, and adjourn afterwards to dine together,
Dutch treat, in a restaurant such as L'Etoile or Antoine's; or
later, at Leonard Woolf's Victoria Square flat, with dinner at
the Queen's Hotel Restaurant.

For the first twelve years, the Club met as frequently as eight times a year. In June 1931, we find Molly writing to Vanessa proposing to have a Centenary Dinner at the MacCarthys' in July; this would indicate that an average of eight meetings a year had occurred since February 1920, a club customarily reckoning its hundredth anniversary by meetings, not by years. But after 1932, when Lytton Strachey had died, and when a number of members lived at a distance, the Club aimed at three meetings annually, and usually met twice or even only once a year. The difficulty of finding free times when everybody could get together, especially with the members scattered geographically, forced that reduction.

It was an unwritten law that Memoir Club papers were not to be mentioned outside of meetings, which gave the members complete freedom to say what they pleased. Naturally, the meetings were very gay, one whoop of laughter after another. Papers had to be only personal recollections; none were permitted on topics requiring research. Because most members wanted to take their manuscripts home with them, no archives have been preserved, not even a list of topics. By 1945, when Dermod MacCarthy became a member, there would be two readers at a meeting (Molly noted in scheduling the February meeting that at the previous one '3 were too many'), and the older member would read first, followed by the younger. Papers lasted usually about twenty minutes, though if the subject and treatment were amusing, they might stretch an hour or more. Dermod's first contribution was on memories of his father, with Desmond and Molly sitting there listening, and Forster was a little miffed because Dermod's paper raised more laughs than his preceding paper had done. The discussion following each paper tended to be on its subject, not on its literary quality, diverging into associated memories (after the death of Lytton Strachey, especially memories of Cambridge), and breaking up the group into small tête-à-têtes.

Molly's proposed list of members, quoted above, should be amended to include Leonard Woolf, Lytton Strachey, and E. M. Forster as charter members and to exclude Proby and possibly Waterlow, who never joined. Members added to the Memoir Club over the years included, besides Lydia Lopokova Keynes, Jane Bussy, and Dermod MacCarthy, already mentioned, Frances Marshall Partridge, Adrian Stephen, Oliver

Strachey (years after the death of Lytton), David and Angelica
Bell Garnett, Quentin and Anne Olivier Bell, Julia Strachey
Gowing, Sebastian Sprott, and Sir Denis Proctor. There may
have been others, but these at least are documented by Mrs.
Partridge, the survivors appearing in her list of Memoir Club
members in 1959.

Mary MacCarthy wrote both for the Club and for publication. *A Pier and A Band,* her only novel, which came out
in 1918 during the Novel Club year, is dedicated to her younger
sister Cecilia, 'who likes a little quiet reading before she goes to
sleep'. That was also one of Molly's pleasures in life; she
records, in a letter of December 1941, looking forward to a
bleak wartime Christmas, solaced, however, by reading in bed
with a hot water bottle every night. *A Pier and A Band* was republished in 1931 by Martin Secker in the New Adelphi Library, with an excellent brief introductory letter by David
Garnett; then that edition was reissued by Hamish Hamilton in
1950. In his prefatory letter, David Garnett calls this novel
'Tchehov's "Cherry Orchard" in an English setting'—except
that Mrs. MacCarthy, quite unconscious of any such resem-
blance, used only her own recollections and observations as
sources, and that her story falls into two parts, when her heroine
is sent from her Devonshire home to Germany. The decay of the
old world studied in this novel is nevertheless reinforced and
enlarged by the contrasts between the north Devonshire and the
East Prussian country upper-class life; and the theme, now newly
relevant, concerns the preservation of unspoiled country as well
as the old-fashioned values, or lack of values, in the life of the
country aristocracy. These questions were concerns also of her
father's books and those of his cousins, Vaughan and James
George Cornish. Mary MacCarthy's attitudes are ambivalent
on the issues posed: should the estates neighbouring Lynton
be cut up by resort hotels, housing developments, the introduction of a railroad spur, 'a pier and a band' (like Margate
or Brighton)? And, in Germany, should the medieval customs
of petty court aristocracy be modified by a little more modern
democracy and humanity? But on the whole, she approves
of spreading the wealth and privilege to the masses, provided the changes are accomplished with due attention to
beauty and good taste. It is a quiet book, highly readable,

and lightened by humour and exquisitely evocative descriptions.

Her next and best-known book, *A Nineteenth-Century Childhood*, was probably a fruit of the Memoir Club; its opening pages assume an audience of that sort. This little volume, relating the author's memories to the date of Queen Victoria's funeral, is a classic; David Cecil has described it as 'a sort of delicate water-colour in prose, as fresh as it is faultless'.

These first two books were obviously written for the fun of their creation, but Mrs. MacCarthy's later three volumes are not so freely artistic and are more uneven in quality. Some of the essays or stories contained in them are equally brilliant—a few may have been started as Memoir Club contributions— but more are the products of research and are occasioned by less happy motives, the wish to make some money, and perhaps in the case of *Handicaps*, the tragic need to fortify herself against her increasing ill health and deafness.

The first of these three, *Fighting Fitzgerald* (1930), required a great deal of research, which Mrs. MacCarthy appears to have done through the good auspices of the London Library. It consists of four biographical sketches of eighteenth-century characters, in a style almost as if it were intended to rival Strachey's *Eminent Victorians*. Though the sketches were composed in reverse order, according to Molly's preface, they are published in order of chronology: Pope's 'Sporus'; the Earl-Bishop, Frederick Hervey, the 4th Earl of Bristol and Bishop of Derry; Fighting Fitzgerald of County Mayo; and 'Humanity' Martin of Connemara. These were eccentric, notable men. Humanity Martin fought a duel with Fitzgerald, and that is how Mary MacCarthy became interested in that Irish adventurer, related both to the Desmonds and to the Hervey ancestors in the preceding sketches. The shorter chapters on the Herveys are the best written—quite up to Strachey's standards.

Handicaps (1936) studies six famous people who rose above serious physical disabilities to achieve some kind of greatness in writing or in the arts or in politics: Mary Lamb, Beethoven, Arthur Kavanagh, Henry Fawcett, W. E. Henley, and R. L. Stevenson. For some of these chapters Mrs. MacCarthy must have had access to first-hand information from friends and relatives, but she drew her material chiefly from books. These well-written essays, deeply felt and vividly narrated, lack, however, the intimacy of the memoirs. *Handicaps* may be the book that she was projecting in the spring of 1932, when she wrote to the Partridges that she was 'struggling with rather a poor little book, full of ideas that simply peter out, and die away on the lips, or in print. I believe they are all fatuous from the start—but they seem magnificent, in bed, or bath, or bus, or street, given to the winds . . . always rather didactic and idealistic.' Or she may have been thinking of some of the stories and essays in *Festival, etc.*, the smaller collection issued the year after *Handicaps*, or of another novel that she was working on in 1938 and apparently never finished. *Handicaps* and *Festival* are still good reading, but not so distinguished as her first two books.

Her discouragement may have sprung less from her self-critical standards of literary excellence than from her physical condition as she struggled with increasing deafness, caused by otosclerosis, and with other illnesses—her own and her family's—and with fatigue. By the end of that year, 1932, when she had survived the excitements and exertions of Rachel's wedding to Lord David Cecil, she was sufficiently run down to require a stay in a nursing home over Christmas, followed by several months in the south of France, partly at La Souco, the Bussys' home in Roquebrune, and partly at Aix-les-Bains for treatments at the spa. When she returned to London in May, she had recovered from her depression and her colds (though she claimed, perhaps jocularly, that the spa treatments had given her rheumatism in exchange), and was ready to plunge into the social rounds and country visits again—to Ham Spray, to Rockbourne to visit the Cecils, to the Isle of Wight, to Tilton for a meeting of the Memoir Club at the Keyneses' country home and back to London to visit Mrs. MacCarthy Sr., while Desmond had an 'old ruined friend 7' × 4' '(probably Raymond Abbot) visiting at home—there was not room enough in the house for them all at the same time. Molly's story of her near nervous breakdown in 1904 was composed for the Memoir Club about 1934; she must have recalled that experience forcibly during the illness of 1932–3.

What a disaster it was to suffer from deafness when one was married to the most celebrated conversationalist in all of

England, and was oneself an adept at social talk! Molly was courageous and unself-pitying about it, but she was hyper-sensitive to the strain it put upon her friends to converse with her. She would accompany Desmond to dinner-parties, but retreat early leaving him to the long hours of the social evening. More and more, she lived alone, sometimes retiring by herself to country places, and finding her social pleasures in smaller, more intimate visits to and from close friends. Desmond was often with her in these country sojourns and visits, and often away on business or social trips of his own.

Molly used hearing aids; she mentions a trumpet in 1932; another was a box-like receiver that she held on her lap; then there was the pair of earphones, wired like a telephone opera-tor's, that she said made her feel like a horse wearing a check-rein. In June of 1932, when she was staying by herself at a Quaker retreat in Bewdley, Worcestershire, to write on her 'works', she confesses that she can now hear practically nothing at meals and thus particularly enjoys the five-minute silent prayer which follows the Bible reading before dinner. By 1945, hearing in any group, such as the weekend guests at Ham Spray, 'was just impossible'.

She broke down once, in a letter to Ralph Partridge (dated January 12, probably 1944) that reveals touchingly how much her deafness bothered her: 'one *never* gets away from the con-dition and its drawbacks, and *one inflicts it on others*—Talk is constantly stripped of nearly *all charm*, and more and more I find silence best. . . . After all, what describes deafness? *Failure* of hearing. He *failed* to hear. She *failed* to hear.—*Failure!* For years and years, every day a sense of *strain* and *failure*; and though it appears that one is just a mere impenetrable block of wood, or numskull,—all the time the muscular strain is most exhausting; as it is, there is a perpetual natural bourdonne-ment dans la tête, and then the *canned* sound of the instrument *enervant*; and most things being *half* heard, or just missed, one gets an impression of life, as if one were always reading a torn page—guessing at most of it. Well, I am not *heard* physically moaning and groaning as loudly as did *Sir Leslie Stephen*, but it must be said that the condition in a general way, is an utter depressant. . . . But it's *not* as bad as Blindness.' Molly, at that period, was going from Hampton clear across the city once a week to write letters for the patients at the Ophthalmic Hospital in City Road. There she saw the real horrors of blindness.

We should remember, however, in balance against the pains and hardships, the continuous pleasures Molly and Desmond had out of their very full lives. Molly wrote to a friend in 1912 that 'common life' was for her 'full of romance and a prosaic poetry . . . so *absorbing*. . . .' Desmond 'wants fame and excitement and honour—and I want adventures and to write novels and plays, and have several love affairs, and to keep young for five years more, and become an actress, and all sorts of things'. This youthful freshness stayed with her, while her hair turned grey and she began to look older than her years, and the children grew up and left home for school and happy marriages and successful professions.

By 1922, with the post-war financial depression and these increasing demands, the MacCarthys began the custom of letting the Wellington Square house while they went on visits or to other quarters at cheaper rent in the country. One such country cottage during the 'twenties was the 'Home Farm' in Oare, Wiltshire, a small ivy-covered house at £30 a year, across the village high street from the Waterlows and close to other friends. Molly and the children were all better off in that country environment. By 1936, again in a depression financially, the MacCarthys began planning to let the London house permanently and find more rural quarters within commuting distance of the city. This they accomplished in 1940, when—war or no war—they moved house in late spring to Garrick's Villa on the north bank of the Thames in Hampton, just beyond the high street and the Palace. They occupied a seven-room ground-floor flat in that house, with a garden behind it 'shaded at one end by two magnificent Spanish chestnuts, probably planted in Garrick's day. . . . Then plunging under the road by a grotto-like tunnel,' one emerged 'on a smooth lawn sloping down to the tame brown rippling Thames'. Desmond and their guests enjoyed swimming and boating off this 'Lido'. Servants, of course, by this time were reduced to the cook and the occasional gardener. Thyrza, the London house-parlourmaid of the 'twenties and 'thirties, who got to look more and more like a fox with an apron on—perhaps *was* 'Lady Into Fox'—had given place to Blanche, who persisted to the end, and whom Molly eventually came to call privately 'Carte Blanche', with her sulky temper and inhospitable ways and unimaginative cooking just when company arrived and Molly wanted everything to feel festive. Nevertheless, Blanche had 'enormous merits'; she would 'wash and sew; mend up old Mr. Abbot's ragged coats . . . relining this and cleaning that, and using the heavy iron like a tailor . . . always on ladders putting up curtains; and dispatching parcels of cake for birthdays I don't remember . . . most ungrasping over money and that is a great merit.'

One of the most brilliant pieces of Mary MacCarthy's writing is her unpublished Memoir Club paper, 'Dire Februaries', which she intended to be the first chapter of 'The Bird Is On the Wing'. In it one finds an intimate view of Desmond and Molly at Garrick's Villa weathering the awful nightly bombings that swept up the Thames in the autumn of 1940, and on into the 'grim Februaries' of 1941 and 1942, as the Nazis tried to locate the Vickers factory hidden near them. Writing in February 1942, she begins with the contrast between her mother's diary entry for January 22, 1901 (also written by the Thames) ruing the end of the Victorian era and apprehending vague, mild changes for the worse, with what Molly, her daughter, must record of present frightfulness. She summarizes the crescendo of horrors in twentieth-century history, the Great War, the Russian Revolution, the rise of Fascism, the 'phony war' of 1939–40, and concentrates on the present scene. She and Desmond had been visiting the Cecils in September 1939, when the ghastly news was brought to them. 'Peace there and then went away . . . we forsook the sunny garden with the cool dew still fresh on the roses and the grass, and went sorrowfully down the path . . .; to those of us who still held the poignant memories of the Great War, it was as though we had caught again a sickness we had had before . . . ; a bitterness, as of poison,' rose in her throat. This was 'the failure of all our educated ardent hopes and the reasonable intellectual arguments for a workable pacifism. . . .' Now she remembers herself sitting by the 'small glow' of a coal fire in her writing-room at Garrick's Villa, in February 1941, at dusk after tea, she writing and Desmond doing a chess puzzle to avoid 'worrying about the news'. Desmond asks her what she has been writing and she recapitulates, ending with the 'regrets for Queen Victoria's simpler days and safer political times'. 'Yes,' Desmond replies, 'Queen Victoria was like a heavy granite paper weight keeping a lot of papers down. When she was gone they all began flutter- ing about everywhere.' He speaks 'between cigarette puffs, looking up from the chess board, but holding on with finger and thumb to a bishop'. She continues the story of their nightly routine—putting up the blackout curtains, dining, bedtime, the raid (the explosions wake even her in her deafness), sitting up through it with the Scottish sea-captain and his lady folks from the upstairs flat, who are given refuge in the MacCarthys' kitchen with unlimited cups of tea. Then the sunrise, the morning trip to the railway station, and the peaceful sunny garden by the Thames.

The narrative framework is filled out with a stream of consciousness of memories, reflections, and digressions, which actually carry the weight of the ideas. She imagines the plight of soldiers and sailors, the bombing out in fact of London friends and acquaintances and tradesmen, the harassments of daily living in wartime, such as rationing—ideas and feelings great and small, tragic and humorous, now choking with excite- ment, again boringly tedious. She begins a three-page con- clusion, which will discuss briefly the still more '*formidable*' experiences of the deepening war between that February and this of 1942: 'Nothing has happened just here, since that Blitz, until a January night in 1942, when a bomb landed within two yards of the house in the garden, and all the windows of the east side of the house cracked and burst into splinters.' 'The tall poplar trees that grow in a long row' on 'the lower lawn down by the river', where an oil bomb also fell, 'toss and sway and shiver so expressively in the winds', that 'in fancy' they have 'seemed to me since then on windy days to be for ever going over the adventure to one another, whispering, shivering, swaying and tossing, as they make a saga of their own small part in that fiery night, charred by flames, down by the river'. The whole essay is framed by brief word-pictures of the Thames, in peace, and at war.

The next untitled chapter of 'The Bird Is On the Wing' (a four-page corrected typescript which would serve as a bridge to the chapter on her early married life in Suffolk) Molly sets as a meditation on a June morning in 1945, when, waking in the 'spare room' at home, alone, she appreciates fully the glorious freshness of the summer's day, its peace and quiet, and feels 'in our own house the first sense of positive rapture that there was no more war'—no guns going off. She imagines the morning day-dreams of the troops coming home to live their own lives free from danger; which brings her, 'pillowed unworthily comfortably', to her own dream 'of bringing out another short book of memories that I would like now to achieve before I go hence. I had succeeded just with one book— "A Nineteenth-Century Childhood," but alas! so long ago! "Too short-winded to count at all," I imagined a cross critic saying to me, priding himself on his candour. "You have only been like one of those obsolete little Victorian round nursery musical boxes . . . with a scrap picture on its top and a child's handle to turn and tinkle out its gurgling tune, say, of 'Wandering Willy,' or one with a nostalgic refrain like your own, 'Home was home then, my dears—happy for a child.' Oh, you have been too short-winded to count!" ' But she must make 'one more practical effort yet, surely! . . . The sudden realization of the extraordinary shortness of the remaining time on earth is frightening, grave.' She recalls Bishop Crichton's dictum, 'Nothing is so pernicious as diffusion. What you need is a definite object and perseverance.' 'At least I had completed "Dire Februaries" from the midst of the Hitler war. . . .'

The remaining years of Molly's life, however, were full of great satisfactions, as well as worries, principally worry over Desmond's overwork and asthma. Her two sons were happily married and well settled in farming and medicine. The grandchildren were a constant source of delight. There were honours for Desmond, including the knighthood in 1951. As president of P.E.N., he was often abroad, but Molly less often left home, though she still visited at Ham Spray occasionally and more frequently went to see her married children. There were often guests at Garrick's Villa. In June 1952, she accompanied Desmond to Cambridge to see him receive the honorary degree of LL.D., and there he was suddenly taken ill and died on June 7, two days after the ceremony. She was left really alone.

She moved into a smaller flat at Garrick's Villa, and by August was able to visit the Cecils and in September the Partridges. She would not be 'like a Mrs. Gummidge *widow* (so unlike anything to do with Desmond!)—I am only an ordinary Molly, much as usual—but now nearly "over" as one says of all the garden produce'. Yet she writes in November from Garrick's Villa, 'All the time here just now every evening I feel the intolerable sense that Desmond *can't* come in the room; and that that is what I want and can't possibly have.' Her last visit away from home was to the Isle of Wight, to sit daily with 'lonely old Mr. Abbot'. In November 1953, she had a heart attack, and slowly faded away at home, dying peacefully on December 28th. So passed away an important spirit from the fading inner circle of the Bloomsbury Group. 'She was indeed *une âme bien née*, generous, sensitive, honest, brave, and with a youthful fineness of spirit that neither age nor trouble could tarnish.'

7

Epilogue

WE HAVE followed the fortunes of these ladies associated with the Bloomsbury Group over a time-span of more than a century, bridging the history between the fading of the Clapham Sect and the decline of Bloomsbury proper. Descendants of these families and of the other families associated with them continue to play distinguished roles in the culture of Britain, but close family associations among them have somewhat loosened. The children now tend to marry outside of the group, and the sense of the clan has passed into history.

What, we should ask, has been the lasting influence of these remarkable women? For one thing, I would suggest, they may be thanked for helping to promote the status of women and the cultivation of a more civilized society (which we often still lack), a society of men and women who live and work together as equals, respecting each other's human traits without regard to sexual stereotyping. For another, they were at least partly responsible for cultivating the creative abilities of their talented offspring. But even more importantly, they awakened and stored their children's active memories, to the point that the final characteristic form of Bloomsbury as a group became the Memoir Club. Perhaps Mnemosyne was rightly imagined as female.

One tends to think of the Bloomsbury Group as an *avant-garde* for their day in the arts, in morals, and in political, social and economic trends of thought; and so they were. Their contributive influence is still felt in movements such as the liberation of women and the search for world peace. But their own perspectives on history were so broad, so long, and so omnipresent in their published works that the further they recede from us in time, the more middle-of-the-road or even conservative they appear. Their classical, truth-loving humanity, enriched by affection, laughter, and enjoyment of life, which was their characteristic spirit, was at least in part owing to their heritage from these ancestresses.

NOTES

Page 7

The Pattle Sisters: This chapter, composed in 1954, is cited as an unpublished source in Brian Hill's *Julia Margaret Cameron: A Victorian Family Portrait* (London: Peter Owen, 1973). It came to Mr. Hill's attention through members of the Pattle family, who had erroneously dubbed it 'a thesis'. Mr. Hill's book is the fullest and most entertaining narrative of the story briefly given in this chapter.

born in Calcutta: Three other children in the family died in infancy or early childhood: James Roche Mitford, b. Feb. 8, 1813, at Calcutta, d. Oct. 13, 1813, at Murshidabad; Eliza Julia, b. Apr. 3, 1814, d. May 30, 1818, at sea; and Harriott Trevor Charlotte, b. Mar. 3, 1828, at the Cape of Good Hope, d. June 1828, at Calcutta. From Family Records of the Indian Branch of the Pattle family in the possession of the late Mrs. Jane Gordon-Wright of Montreal (hereafter referred to as Family Records), and the memorial tablet to James and Adeline Pattle in St. Giles' Church, Camberwell. See also *The Bengal Obituary* (Calcutta: Holmes & Co., 1851), p. 119.

Mar. 19, 1829: From Family Records and the memorial tablet at Camberwell.

'actually plain': Laura Gurney, Lady Troubridge, *Memories and Reflections* (London: Wm. Heinemann, 1925), p. 7.

Page 8

'to death': *Victorian Photographs of Famous Men and Fair Women*, with introductions by Virginia Woolf and Roger Fry (New York: Harcourt, Brace, 1926), p. 1.

'their hands': W. H. Carey, *The Good Old Days of Honourable John Company* (Calcutta: R. Cambray & Co., 1906), I, 158.

rank of Factor: *Bengal Kalendar . . . 1800*, p. 5.

public affairs: He chaired the town meeting to organize the Retirement Annuity Fund for Civil Servants and served on the executive committee for this Fund; he helped prepare the farewell 'address' and Ball and Supper for the Marquess of Hastings; and he was a leading spirit in the enterprise to encourage with a premium the inauguration of steamship service between London and Calcutta (*Selections from Calcutta Gazettes*, V, 431–2, 500, 507, and 565).

rupees a month: *Bengal and Agra Guide and Gazetteer* (1842), Pt. 2, Appendix, p. 131.

Page 9
junior civil servants: William Tayler, *Thirty-Eight Years in India* (London, 1882), I, 338–49.

planning to import: H. E. A. Cotton, *Calcutta Old and New* (Calcutta: W. Newman & Co., 1907), p. 189.

'American importation': J. H. Siddons (pseud. Stocqueler), *Memoirs of a Journalist* (Bombay, 1873), pp. 103–4.

ill-treated her: 'I assure you,' said old General Smyth, 'it astonishes me sometimes to think what a lot of scamps I have had to do with in my time. For instance there was a fellow called Pattle whom I knew very well when I was on the Governor-General's staff—Jim Pattle . . . as big a scamp as ever you saw, and a bad fellow in every way. Behaved very ill to his wife too, but she was devoted to him, and when—well, when anything went wrong, he used to say that it *couldn't be helped now*, and she was quite satisfied and forgave him again and again.' See Dame Ethel Mary Smyth, *Impressions That Remained*, 2nd ed. (New York: Knopf, 1946), p. 476.

'bewailed her': *Bengal Obituary*, p. 31. Another white marble tablet was placed by one of the Pattle daughters in the dispensary at Garden Reach Road, in 1846—'To the Memory of Adeline Pattle, this Dispensary is dedicated by her daughter, assuaging grief for a lost mother, by relieving the wants of the poor' (ibid., p. 316).

Page 10
'housewifely arts': M. S. Watts, *George Frederic Watts; the Annals of an Artist's Life* (London: Macmillan, 1912), I, 129. After she had concluded her educational task for her granddaughters, Madame de l'Etang turned her attention to the great-grandchildren. Watts 'remembered seeing [her], when upwards of eighty, down on her knees in a passage in the [Prinsep] house in Chesterfield Street, keenly interested in playing a game of chuck-halfpenny with her great-grandsons' (ibid., I, 129). 'The old ideas survived with Mme. de l'Etang in the old house at Versailles, where she had her circle and her mild card-playing every night. One evening, when being dressed

for her little party, she leaned back in her chair, said to the faithful Annette, "I am tired", and died' (*The Connoisseur*, July 1925, p. 178). This occurred in 1866, when she was ninety-eight years old (*The Times*, Oct. 3, 1910, p. 13).

for matrimony: Gordon N. Ray, ed., *The Letters and Private Papers of William Makepeace Thackeray* (Cambridge: Harvard University Press, 1945), I, 189, 192, 208, 230–1, 237, and 266. See also p. 267: 'I dine today with the Pattles and shall meet pretty Theodosia—I wish she had £11325 in the 3 per cents—I would not hesitate above two minutes in popping that question. . . .' It is possible that Maria's middle name was Theodosia. Thackeray's letter to his mother, Dec. 23, 1833, a passage of which has been destroyed (ibid., I, 272), might be interpreted thus: 'I had a long letter from Mrs. Pattle [who is going to India &] who evidently desires to make a [daughter's match]—I wrote her back word that I was [ruined and wait to] see how she will bear the news—' Thackeray had just lost the sum mentioned above in the ruin of certain banks in Bengal.

'male sex in Calcutta': Lord Curzon, *British Government in India* (London: Cassell & Co., 1925), I, 220, referring to Christina Pringle, 'Letters from Calcutta and Jessore in 1829–30', *Bengal: Past and Present* (1909), IV, 469.

'loves and hates': Troubridge, p. 38.

Page 11
'a Miss Pattle': Hon. Frederick Leveson-Gower, *Bygone Years* (London: John Murray, 1905), p. 159.

three small daughters: Mackenzie, I, 25–76. According to Family Records, the Mackenzie daughters, Adeline Anne, Mary Julia, and Rose Prinsep, married respectively Maj.-Gen. Henry Hoseason, Maj. Herbert Mackworth Clogstoun, and (1) Lieut. David Arnot, (2) Capt. Francis Pictet, all officers of the Madras Army, associated with their father. The Clogstouns both died young, leaving three young daughters, who were sent to their great-aunts Julia and Sara in England. Little Blanche Clogstoun, 'with long fair hair and dressed in deep mourning', won the heart of G. F. Watts, who asked permission to adopt her. She stayed with her aunt Sara and Watts, while the other two girls were brought up by their aunt Julia. See Troubridge, pp. 8–10. Lady Troubridge concludes this story: Blanche 'became my dearest friend, and eventually married Herbert Somers Cocks, a young officer in the Coldstream Guards, and heir to the Barony of Somers, to which his son later succeeded'. This means, to anticipate the story, that Blanche was not only a great-niece of Virginia Pattle, Countess Somers, but also a niece by marriage.

eldest Pattle sister: See her niece Julia Jackson Stephen's account of her in the *D.N.B.*; also Leslie Stephen's article in the *D.N.B.* on Charles Hay Cameron.

Page 12

Sir Edward Ryan: Hon. Emily Eden, *Letters From India* (London, 1872), I, 115.

famine relief: Helmut Gernsheim, *Julia Margaret Cameron: Her Life and Photographic Art* (London: The Fountain Press, 1948), p. 12.

Persian scholar: A. J. Arbuthnot, 'Henry Thoby Prinsep', *D.N.B.* (1921–2), XVI, 392–5. One of Thoby's brothers, Charles Robert Prinsep, was advocate-general in Calcutta, and the owner of Belvidere, the great house five miles outside of Calcutta, across the river Hooghly, which had been built by Warren Hastings and which Prinsep eventually sold to government for the Residency of the Lieut.-Gov. of Bengal. Another brother, James Prinsep, was highly respected as a scholar and Director of the Mint in Calcutta. Prinsep's Ghaut was built as a memorial to him.

live in London: First in Hyde Park Gardens, then at 9 Chesterfield Street, or when Sara was with her grandmother in Paris, he would stay with his mother, old Mrs. John Prinsep, at 6 Great Cumberland Street.

in 1830: Family Records. See also Lieut.-Col. D. G. Crawford, *Roll of the Indian Medical Service 1615–1930* (London: W. Thacker & Co., 1930), p. 102: John Jackson, b. Nov. 17, 1804; B.A. Univ. College, London; M.B. (1829) St. Catherine's College, Cambridge, from which university he was granted the M.D. in 1855. He was a Fellow of the Royal College of Surgeons (1844, original list). He was made presiding surgeon in Calcutta, Mar. 1, 1847, and retired from the service of the Honourable Company on Dec. 31, 1855. Member of the Royal College of Physicians, London, 1856, and Fellow, 1859. He died at Brighton on Mar. 31, 1887. He was author of *Forms of Tetanus in India*, 1856.

the liver: *Bengal and Agra Annual Guide and Gazetteer*, 1841; *The East-India Register*, 'Bengal', 1849, p. 183, and 1851, p. 193; *Calcutta Literary Gleaner*, May 1843, pp. ii, xiii, and xvii, and Feb. 1844.

'Indians in Calcutta': Gerald Ritchie, *The Ritchies in India* (London: John Murray, 1920), p. 131.

Director of the Company: Family Records, and Burke's *Family Records*, 1897, p. 56.

Page 13

appointed in 1834: *East-India Register and Army List* (1849), 'Bengal', p. 11.

defamation: Tayler, I, 305–6, 310, and 317.

some years before: After 1850, H. V. Bayley resumed his career in Calcutta as Superintendent of Stamps and Stationery and deputy secretary to the Board of Customs, Salt and Opium (*E.-I. Register*, 1851, 'Bengal', p. 11). This appointment put him under the Indian Law Commission, and most of the rest of his career had to do with the administration of the law courts. In 1852–53, however, he was collector of the 24-Parganas, the district east of Calcutta, and by 1855 was junior secretary of the Board of Revenue, living in Garden Reach. He was made judge of the Hooghly district, west of Calcutta, 1856–8, judge in the native courts in Calcutta, 1860–2, and judge of the Supreme Court in Calcutta, 1863–73. He died in Calcutta in 1873 and is buried in the Lower Circular Road Cemetery. He was remembered as 'the last of the "Old Brigade" of *quihyes* to smoke a hookah in the Bengal Club' (Cotton, p. 582).

'wonder for you!': Ray, I, 391.

'Thackeray': Ritchie, p. 131.

Page 14

'painful disease': *Bengal Obituary* (1851), p. 31.

'at Camberwell': Ibid., p. 31. According to Gen. Smyth, he was to have been buried beside his mother in Marylebone Church (Smyth, p. 476).

Julia's photographs: Woolf, introd., *Victorian Photographs*, p. 1.

'his daughters': E. F. Benson, *As We Were; A Victorian Peepshow* (London: Longmans, Green & Co., 1931), pp. 76–7.

Page 15

'go out of India': Smyth, pp. 476–7.

'aged 52': *Bengal Obituary*, p. 31.

'Pattle girls': Ray, II, 232.

Dalrymple, B.C.S.: Burke's *Peerage* (1949), p. 538.

Page 16

'into my hair': Ray, II, 325.

'lasted long': H. G. Rawlinson, ed., *Personal Reminiscences of Augusta Becher, 1830–1888* (London: Constable & Co., 1930), pp. 27–8. Uncle George Haldimand, who had married Thoby's oldest sister, belonged to the great Swiss banking house, which had occupied, with Mr. John Prinsep, the houses in Leadenhall Street that eventually became the India House.

Page 17
'two bulls': Cotton, p. 284.

'differ with him': Violet Dickinson, ed., *Miss Eden's Letters* (London: Macmillan & Co., 1919). p. 320.

'his nature': Watts, I, 123.

'scene of tumult': Troubridge, p. 20.

the year before: Watts, I, 121–3: An acquaintance, Mr. Fleming, whom Watts met at Holland House, raved to him about the beauty of Miss Virginia Pattle, then living with the Prinseps in Chesterfield Street. A few days later Watts 'happened to pass two ladies walking with a little boy', doubtless Sara, Virginia, and young Arthur; Watts recognized them from Fleming's description, repaired to Fleming for an introduction, and was soon on friendly terms with the Prinseps. His first portrait of Virginia, 'in delicate silver point', shows her as she had looked that first morning in her long grey cloak.
Watts's notebooks Nos. 1 and 2 are full of 'studies . . . done for the most part from Mrs. Prinsep, Lady Dalrymple, Mrs. Jackson . . . and her three daughters', some of which are also reproduced in Mrs. Watts's biography of her husband. See Introduction to No. 21 (Sara) and No. 22 (Sophia), of the Vasari Society, *Reproductions of Drawings of Old Masters* (Oxford: Oxford University Press, 1920), 2nd series, part 1. Incidentally, Arthur Prinsep as a boy was bribed by Watts to keep his hair uncut so that he could model for drawings from which Watts later painted his 'Sir Galahad', 'Aspiration', 'Hyperion', and 'The Red Cross Knight with Una'. Holman Hunt also used one of these drawings for his picture of 'Christ Among the Doctors' (Watts, I, 158).

'thirty years': Watts, I, 128–9.

'delightful conversation': Ibid., I, 128, 203.

Page 18
songs to him: Ibid., I, 159–60, 201–4.

'half the world': Troubridge, p. 47. For an imaginative reconstruction of the Prinseps' and Watts's life at Little Holland House, see also Ronald Chapman, *The Laurel and the Thorn, A Study of G. F. Watts* (London: Faber & Faber, 1945); and Wilfrid Blunt, '*England's Michelangelo*' (London: Hamish Hamilton, 1975).

Page 19

devoted friendship: Anne Thackeray, Lady Ritchie, *From Friend to Friend*, ed. Emily Ritchie (London: John Murray, 1919), pp. 2-7. Emily Tennyson began her long correspondence with Julia Cameron in a note thanking her for a happy day spent at Kew Gardens in June 1852. Julia had won the Tennysons' hearts by her aid when their first child was born dead the preceding Easter.

at Bromley: Gernsheim, pp. 17, 19.

'a pleasant party': *Letters of Anne Thackeray Ritchie*, ed. Hester Ritchie (London: John Murray, 1924), p. 62.

'pulpit cushion': Hester Thackeray Fuller and V. Hammersley, comp., *Thackeray's Daughter; Some Recollections* (Dublin, 1951), pp. 110-11.

Page 20

Guest's: Lady Ritchie, *From Friend to Friend*, pp. 12-15.

' "Holy Family" ': Wilfrid Ward, *Aubrey deVere, A Memoir* (London: Longmans, Green & Co., 1904), p. 162. However, a note from Caroline Norton to Henry Taylor, probably from the early 1850's, suggests that she invented the term Pattledom: 'I have not yet been to what I call the Kingdom of Pattledom (and what Mr. Stirling calls the Battlefield) at Little Holland House. . . .' See Una Taylor, *Guests and Memories* (London: Humphrey Milford, Oxford University Press, 1924), p. 379.

'tower in between': Gernsheim, p. 17; and Agnes Grace Weld, *Glimpses of Tennyson and Some of His Relations and Friends* (London: Williams and Norgate, 1903), pp. 73-5.

'healthy lea': Lady Ritchie, *From Friend to Friend*, p. 20.

'incident and interest': Wilfrid Ward, *Men and Matters* (London: Longmans, Green & Co., 1914), pp. 251, 257-8.

Page 21

'for six months': Ibid., p. 259.

Page 22

'should have been': Troubridge, pp. 34-5.

'left of you': Gernsheim, pp. 25-6.

Father Time: Weld, p. 77.

Page 23
'look grand?': Ward, *Men and Matters*, pp. 260–1.

would be worth: Gernsheim, p. 27.

Page 25
'painters in photography': Ibid., pp. 28–9, 31–2, 34, 55, 57, and 61.

gave to the Prinseps: Watts, I, 251–65.

'nineteenth century': Ibid., I, 298. Tennyson, passing the great rosemary bushes in the kitchen garden of the Briary, would rub the leaves through his fingers and quote the old folk saying, 'Where rosemary flourishes, there the woman of the house bears rule.' (Weld, p. 83.)

Page 26
'Empress of India': Weld, p. 85.

'their farewell': Watts, I, 301.

'a cow': Woolf, introd., *Victorian Photographs*, p. 8.

Madonna Mary: Watts, I, 301.

'marriages and deaths': Una Taylor, pp. 384–5.

Page 27
'dear Mrs. Cameron': Fuller and Hammersley, p. 155.

a short time: Troubridge, pp. 43–4.

extravagant than ever: Ibid., pp. 52–3.

George Corrie: *The Bengal Obituary*, p. 119.

Page 28
spiritual: Or perhaps one should say least imaginative and most conventional and sentimental. A little note from her to William Tayler in Calcutta, 1844, the only published bit of writing from her hand, gives something of the flavour of her nature (Tayler, I, 353). See also her son-in-law Leslie Stephen's letters to her, published in F. W. Maitland, *Leslie Stephen* (London: Duckworth & Co., 1906), pp. 314–16. Quentin Bell, who has had to read a great many of his great-grandmother's letters, concludes that 'Mrs. Jackson's . . . display the dull side of the Pattles; their silliness, their gush, their cloying sweetness, their continual demands for affection and with it a mawkish vein, a kind of tender gloating over disease and death.'

(Quentin Bell, *Virginia Woolf, A Biography*. Vol. I: *Virginia Stephen, 1882–1912*, London: Hogarth Press, 1972, p. 17.)

'increased with age': Watts, I, 129.

'three beautiful daughters': Lady Ritchie, *From Friend to Friend*, p. 19.

'took her advice': Troubridge, pp. 50–1.

early manhood: *The Bengal Obituary*, p. 119; Burke's *Family Records* (1897), p. 56. Brian Hill, however, records only four Bayley children; it is likely that the number nine is in error and refers to grandchildren.

visits together: Rawlinson, pp. 186, 201–17.

March 1873: Burke's *Family Records* (1897), p. 56.

Tipperah and Calcutta: Dalrymple's first appointments were in Tipperah, the wild region across the Bay of Bengal, where he rose to be joint magistrate and deputy collector, and then in Calcutta, as under-secretary to the Government of Bengal. After an interval from 1853 to 1859, which he possibly spent in England, he appears in India again as deputy judge and judge of the Hooghly District, then as judge and commissioner for the division of Bhagalpur and the Santal Parganas in Bihar (1863–73), with two years (1867–8) as commissioner for the Patna division, a little farther up the Ganges. See *E.-I. Register and Army List* (1849), 'Bengal', p. 14; (1851), 'Bengal,' p. 3; and *Appointments in Bengal and Their Holders . . . 1850 . . . to 1902* (Calcutta: Bengal Secretariat Press, 1903), pp. 203, 82–3, and 112.

Page 29
'artist's eye': Watts, I, 155, 157.

'incredibly old': Troubridge, p. 21.

Lady Somers as Beauty: Woolf, introd., *Victorian Photographs*, pp. 2–3.

Page 30
Watts's studio: Watts, I, 125–6.

'her watchcase': Ibid., I, 123.

'perfectly beautiful woman': Troubridge, p. 57.

Page 31
'expressive': Watts, I, 122. This simplicity of taste was inherited by the Pattle daughters, especially by Alice Prinsep Gurney, who

with her beauty, wit, and social skill was one of the leaders of the Marlborough House set. Mrs. Gurney used to cause a sensation at the Ascot meetings 'by her arrival in the Royal Enclosure in a simple tussore dress or a white poplin, stuffs which were never heard of for dresses at a race-meeting, but which, on her, looked just right'. To her sense of the appropriate was also due the fashion of country clothes—'short pleated skirts and jerseys, the jersey being a thing unheard of, and invented and popularised by her.' (Troubridge, p. 13.)

'to Italy': Benson, p. 77.

'shrewdness': Troubridge, p. 58.

'hospitality': Benson, pp. 80–1.

'roses': Watts, II, 124.

'to another': *The Times*, Oct. 3, 1910, p. 13.

Page 33
'carefully': Noel Annan, *Leslie Stephen: His Thought and Character in Relation to His Time* (Cambridge: Harvard University Press, 1952), p. 73.

'singing': Ritchie, *Letters of Anne Thackeray Ritchie*, p. 129.

'impression on Julia': Annan, p. 74.

Somersetshire: Bell, *Virginia Woolf: A Biography*, I, 20.

Page 34
distress: Leslie Stephen, *Social Rights and Duties: Addresses to Ethical Societies* (London: Swann Sonnenschein & Co. and New York: Macmillan & Co., 1896), II, 255–7.

Page 35
'substantial reasons': Maitland, pp. 320–1.

Page 36
Julia's social character: The letters are preserved in the Berg Collection of the New York Public Library; some of them have been partially published in the Norton edition of Lowell's letters and quoted in Martin Duberman's *James Russell Lowell* (Boston: Houghton Mifflin, 1966).

William Rothenstein: In *Men and Memories . . . 1872–1900* (New York: Coward-McCann, Inc., 1935), I, 97–8.

Page 37
'snap of you': Leonard Woolf, *Beginning Again*, p. 51.

'exodus to Cornwall': Bell, I, 30.

Page 38
'far off': Maitland, p. 384.

'black hat': Bell, I, 33-4.

'gratitude': Maitland, p. 431.

Page 39
'burnt out': Bell, I, 38-9.

Page 40
'before he arrived': Annan, pp. 99-101.

'fiction of fact': Bell, I, 18, and Annan, p. 102. Annan's mention of Mrs. Ambrose and Mrs. Hilbery as further fictional portraits of Julia Stephen can be true only in part: Mrs. Ambrose was apparently modelled on Vanessa; see Clive Bell's letter to Virginia Woolf, in Bell, I, 210; and Mrs. Hilbery is a portrait chiefly of Aunt Anny Thackeray Ritchie.

Page 44
'off hand': M. S. Watts, *G. F. Watts*, II, 60.

Page 46
conscious mind: Aileen Pippett, *The Moth and the Star: A Biography of Virginia Woolf* (Boston: Little, Brown and Co., 1955), p. 231.

Page 47
'such a presence': *The Selected Letters of Henry James*, ed. with an introd. by Leon Edel (New York: Farrar, Straus & Cudahy, 1955), p. 149.

Page 51
subjects born at sea: Unpublished 'Memoirs' of Jane Maria Grant Lady Strachey, pp. 1-2. All facts and quotations in the following narrative of Lady Strachey's life are derived from this 172-page typescript, unless otherwise noted. Since about one-fourth of it was selected and published by Leonard Woolf in the *Nation and the Athenaeum*, in four instalments during 1924, entitled 'Some Recollections of a Long Life', this account will use, so far as relevant, material in the Memoirs not contained in those portions or hitherto stressed by the published accounts of Lady Strachey mentioned above.

Page 54
four miles: Curzon, *British Government in India*, I, 22–5, and II, map facing p. 10.

Page 57
Hindu widows: For years Grant had studied the persistent custom of suttee, from which all liberal Englishmen shrank with loathing, but which could not be further legislated against, only around. As he said in his closing speech in support of the bill, July, 1856: 'If he knew, certainly, that but one little girl would be saved from the horrors of Bramacharia by the passing of this Act, he would pass it for her sake. If he believed the contrary, that the Act would be wholly a dead letter, he would pass it for the sake of the English name.' W. S. Seton-Kerr, *Grant of Rothiemurchus* (London: John Murray, 1899), p. 34.

Page 58
'Koompanee': A. C. Hare, *Story of Two Noble Lives* (London: George Allen, 1893), II, 466.

Page 59
Lancaster Gate in London: This Alipore residency was the house referred to in Chapter 2 as belonging to Charles Robert Prinsep, who sold it to the government in 1854. Gradually it assumed the look of a Renaissance palace, but in J. P. Grant's reign it still lacked the wings, verandas, and cloisters that later accrued to it. When Pippa Strachey visited there in 1901, it looked like a great two-storey wedding cake, sitting high on a vaulted basement, with a sweeping broad staircase up to the first-floor front entrance. The high windows were round arched on the lower storey, and pilasters and free columns tied together the banks of windows above. The top of the building was ornamented with a classical pediment and statues, and the whole roof was surrounded with a low balustrade.—C. E. Buckland, *Bengal Under the Lieutenant-Governors* (Calcutta: S. K. Lahiri & Co., 1901), II, 1012–21. A flowery account of the grounds as they appeared in the mid-nineteenth century speaks of 'bamboos in fine profusion . . . overarching the roads and lanes', plantains with great leaves like scimitars, shining like green satin, rich lawns, flowering creepers, ponds covered with lotus and waterlilies, banyan and almond trees, and 'even . . . some specimens of the peerless Amherstia'. (Ibid., II, 1019.) For the support of this magnificence, Grant had a salary of 100,000 rupees, three times what he had been earning before.

Page 60
Governor of Bombay: Buckland, I, 235–6.

Page 63

'speak to you?': It should be noted that in the 1880's Jane
Strachey and Browning joined forces, with others, to patronize and
promote the Saturday and Monday Pops. Jane copied in her
Memoirs an unpublished sonnet of Browning's on these concerts,
and appended an unsigned 'Ballade of the Monday Pops', probably
by herself, which is not particularly good, though not much worse
than Browning's, to be sure.

Page 64

became teachers: As schoolmates, and being of the same ages,
Oliver and Pernel Strachey and Billy and Hester Ritchie became
inseparable companions. Everyone rejoiced when Billy married
Margaret Booth, Pernel's best friend at Newnham. (From conversations with the Misses Strachey.)

Page 65

the *Parthia*: It is amusing to read a behind-the-scenes comment
on the Stracheys at this period, in a letter from J. D. Hooker to Asa
Gray, Apr. 8, 1877, arranging this excursion (the letter is preserved
in the Gray Herbarium Library at Harvard): 'What do you say to
my being accompanied to America by General Strachey?—he is
most anxious to come, and would make a splendid physical addition
to our party. We have travelled so much together and so pleasantly
[the latest journey was to Brittany in 1876] that I cannot say him
nay if I would. Of course he expects *no* facilities; but I fancy that
[F. V.] Hayden will be only too glad that so able a man should be
with us. He is an excellent physical explorer, and his (alas yet
unpublished) Exploration and Survey of Kumaon is a first rate piece
of work. He is a most valuable member of the R.S.—a good meteoro-
logist, fair geologist and quite a fellow altogether. Mrs. S., who will
accompany him to America, is a very clever person—a daughter
of Sir J. P. Grant who was Governor of Bengal and late Governor
of Jamaica. Strachey is one of the Government of India of which
Lord Salisbury told me he would miss him more than any other
member.'

'female school teachers': Leonard Huxley, *Life and Letters of Sir
Joseph Dalton Hooker* (London, 1918), II, 207.

Page 66

'*dreadful* clatter': Huxley, II, 210 and 213.

Page 68

'Worst Authors': This and others of the children's magazines are
preserved at Duke University Library.

Page 70
 Forestalled: Published in *The Englishwoman*, Vol. XIV, No. 42 (June, 1912), pp. 252–3.

Page 72
 political status: Millicent Garrett Fawcett, *What I Remember* (London: T. Fisher Unwin Ltd., 1924), pp. 117–18.

Page 73
 'justice and humanity': As quoted in the obituary of Lady Strachey, *The Times*, Dec. 15, 1928, p. 12.

Page 74
 'head of the procession': Fawcett, p. 192.

Page 77
 to 1863: A recent dissertation at the University of Minnesota, 'Anne Thackeray Ritchie and the Victorian Literary Aristocracy', by O. J. H. Preus, available on microfilm, gives a thorough survey of her career and her connections with Victorians as well as especially with Virginia Woolf. Also a London University dissertation, by Jennie Huie, 'Anne Thackeray (afterwards Lady Ritchie)' (1960), is based on hitherto unavailable manuscript materials, and will, I hope, soon appear in published form. A few months after completing this chapter, I read with pleasure a distinguished essay on this same subject which often parallels my conclusions: 'Anne Thackeray Ritchie as the Model for Mrs. Hilbery in Virginia Woolf's *Night and Day*', by Joanne P. Zuckerman, published in the *Virginia Woolf Quarterly*, Spring 1973, Vol. I, No. 3, pp. 32–46.

Page 78
 perceptive remark: *New Statesman and Nation*, Vol. 43 (Mar. 29, 1952), pp. 376–7.

Page 80
 Anny's 'dove': *Thackeray's Daughter*, p. 156 and p. 159.

Page 81
 her *Letters*: *Letters of Anne Thackeray Ritchie*, ed. Hester Ritchie (London: John Murray, 1924).

Page 83
 'into the victoria': *Thackeray's Daughter*, pp. 169–70, citing Mary Warre-Cornish MacCarthy, *A Nineteenth-Century Childhood*.

Page 84
 'governesses': *Chapters From Some Memoirs* (London: Macmillan, 1894), p. 4.

'in letters': 'The Enchanted Organ', in *The Moment and Other Essays* (London: Hogarth Press, 1947), p. 157; reprinted from *The Nation and the Athenaeum*, Vol. 34 (Mar. 15, 1924), p. 836, a review of Lady Ritchie's *Letters*.

unquenchable: Ibid., p. 156.

Page 85
'No wonder!': *Letters*, p. 186 and p. 188.

'hidden from us all': A. I. T. Ritchie, *Tennyson, Ruskin, and Browning* (London: Macmillan, 1892), pp. 35-6.

Page 86
birthday present: *Thackeray's Daughter*, p. 97 and pp. 129-30; see also *Chapters From Some Memoirs*.

Page 88
enough money?: *Toilers and Spinsters and Other Essays* (London: Smith, Elder, & Co., 1874), p. 4.

Mrs. Woolf's style: A splendid example of Virginia Woolf's rhapsodic utterance appears in Quentin Bell's *Virginia Woolf: A Biography* (1972), Vol. I, p. 148. Leonard Woolf parodied this gift exquisitely in his portrait of Virginia (and her sister and friends), in his novel *The Wise Virgins: A Story of Words, Opinions, and a Few Emotions* (London: Edward Arnold, 1914), pp. 125-7.

Page 90
'taken aback' by it: *Thackeray's Daughter*, p. 177.

'tortured girl': *Times Literary Supplement*, Oct. 30, 1919, p. 607.

Page 92
' "lose their tempers" ': Philip Leigh-Smith, *Record of an Ascent: A Memoir of Sir Richmond Thackeray Ritchie* (London: Dillon's University Bookshop, Ltd., 1961), p. 33.

Page 93
other tribute: 'The Enchanted Organ.'

Page 94
'became Molly': Oliver Edwards, 'Talking of Books: In All Centuries', London *Times*, Apr. 22, 1965, p. 15.

Page 95
concludes a letter: To Ralph and Frances Partridge, May 3, 1932.

Page 96
never circulated: See R. Gathorne-Hardy, *Recollections of Logan Pearsall Smith* (New York: Macmillan, 1950), pp. 65–7.

'childbirth?' Edith Wharton writes of Blanche's conversation-stopping utterances in *A Backward Glance* (pp. 237–9), and Aldous Huxley sketches her as Mrs. Cravister in his story, 'Farcical History of Richard Greenow', included in *Limbo* (Chatto & Windus, 1920). The best description of Francis and Blanche Warre-Cornish which I have found is provided in Percy Lubbock's *Shades of Eton* (London: Jonathan Cape, 1929), chapters VIII and IX, pp. 91–112.

Page 110
'far between': ALS Molly MacCarthy to J. M. Keynes, Dec. 31, 1945.

'prinzip': ALS J. M. Keynes to Molly, Jan. 2, 1946.

'our readings': ALS Molly to Keynes, May 26, 1928.

'anxieties': ALS Molly to Keynes, Feb. 4, 1946.

Page 113
Childhood: Appearing first in 1924, dedicated to Desmond Mac-Carthy, it was revised and reissued in the New Adelphi Library in 1929; then republished, first by William Heinemann in 1936, and again by Hamish Hamilton in 1948, including a fulsome introduction by John Betjeman.

later three volumes: *Fighting Fitzgerald . . . and Other Papers* was published by Martin Secker in 1930; *Handicaps. Six Studies* (1936) and *The Festival, etc.* (1937) were published by Longmans, Green.

Page 115
before dinner: ALS to Frances Partridge, June 26, 1932.

Page 116
'sorts of things': ALS Molly to Clive Bell, Apr. and Dec. 1912.

'rippling Thames': Unpublished diary of Frances Partridge.

Page 117
'great merit': ALS Molly to Frances Partridge, May 17, 1953.

Page 120
'garden produce': ALS Molly to Ralph Partridge, July 26, 1952.

'can't possibly have': ALS Molly to Frances Partridge, Nov. 18, 1952.

'tarnish': David Cecil, letter to *The Times*, Jan. 5, 1954, p. 5.

FAMILY TREES

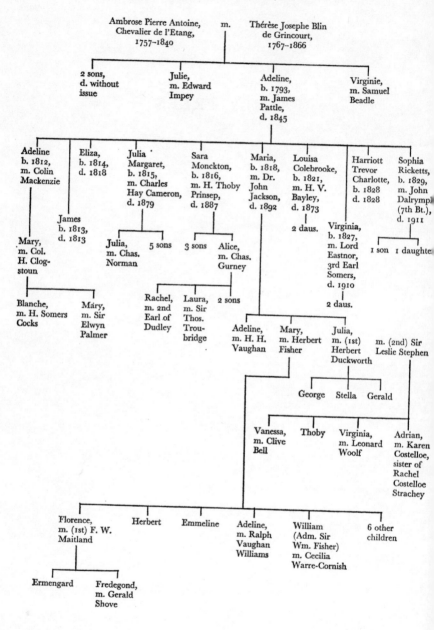

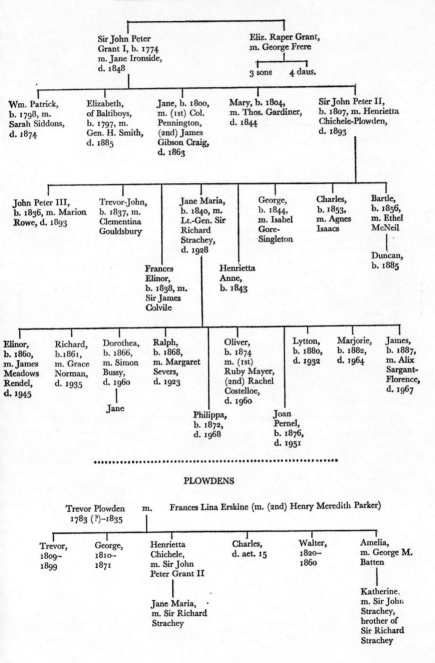

GRANTS of Rothiemurchus and STRACHEYS

Sir John Peter
Grant I, b. 1774
m. Jane Ironside,
d. 1848

Eliz. Raper Grant,
m. George Frere

3 sons   4 daus.

Wm. Patrick,
b. 1798, m.
Sarah Siddons,
d. 1874

Elizabeth,
of Baltiboys,
b. 1797, m.
Gen. H. Smith,
d. 1885

Jane, b. 1800,
m. (1st) Col.
Pennington,
(2nd) James
Gibson Craig,
d. 1863

Mary, b. 1804,
m. Thos. Gardiner,
d. 1844

Sir John Peter II,
b. 1807, m. Henrietta
Chichele-Plowden,
d. 1893

John Peter III,
b. 1836, m. Marion
Rowe, d. 1893

Trevor-John,
b. 1837, m.
Clementina
Gouldsbury

Jane Maria,
b. 1840, m.
Lt.-Gen. Sir
Richard
Strachey,
d. 1928

George,
b. 1844,
m. Isabel
Gore-
Singleton

Charles,
b. 1853,
m. Agnes
Isaacs

Bartle,
b. 1856,
m. Ethel
McNeil

Duncan,
b. 1885

Frances
Elinor,
b. 1838, m.
Sir James
Colvile

Henrietta
Anne,
b. 1843

Elinor,
b. 1860,
m. James
Meadows
Rendel,
d. 1945

Richard,
b.1861,
m. Grace
Norman,
d. 1935

Dorothea,
b. 1866,
m. Simon
Bussy,
d. 1960

Ralph,
b. 1868,
m. Margaret
Severs,
d. 1923

Oliver,
b. 1874
m. (1st)
Ruby Mayer,
(2nd) Rachel
Costelloe,
d. 1960

Lytton,
b. 1880,
d. 1932

Marjorie,
b. 1882,
d. 1964

James,
b. 1887,
m. Alix
Sargant-
Florence,
d. 1967

Jane

Philippa,
b. 1872,
d. 1968

Joan
Pernel,
b. 1876,
d. 1951

PLOWDENS

Trevor Plowden   m.   Frances Lina Erskine (m. (2nd) Henry Meredith Parker)
1783 (?)–1835

Trevor,
1809–
1899

George,
1810–
1871

Henrietta
Chichele,
m. Sir John
Peter Grant II

Charles,
d. aet. 15

Walter,
1820–
1860

Amelia,
m. George M.
Batten

Jane Maria,
m. Sir Richard
Strachey

Katherine,
m. Sir John
Strachey,
brother of
Sir Richard
Strachey

THACKERAYS and RITCHIES

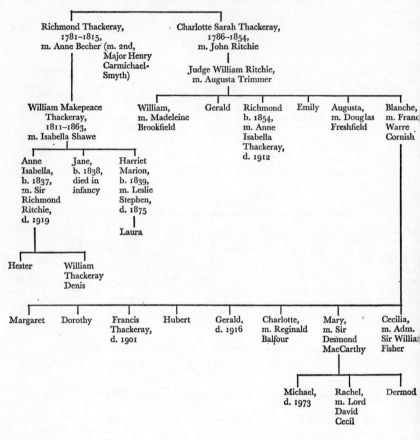

Richmond Thackeray,
1781–1815,
m. Anne Becher (m. 2nd,
Major Henry
Carmichael-
Smyth)

Charlotte Sarah Thackeray,
1786–1854,
m. John Ritchie

Judge William Ritchie,
m. Augusta Trimmer

William Makepeace
Thackeray,
1811–1863,
m. Isabella Shawe

William,
m. Madeleine
Brookfield

Gerald

Richmond
b. 1854,
m. Anne
Isabella
Thackeray,
d. 1912

Emily

Augusta,
m. Douglas
Freshfield

Blanche,
m. Fran
Warre
Cornish

Anne
Isabella,
b. 1837,
m. Sir
Richmond
Ritchie,
d. 1919

Jane,
b. 1838,
died in
infancy

Harriet
Marion,
b. 1839,
m. Leslie
Stephen,
d. 1875

Laura

Hester

William
Thackeray
Denis

Margaret

Dorothy

Francis
Thackeray,
d. 1901

Hubert

Gerald,
d. 1916

Charlotte,
m. Reginald
Balfour

Mary,
m. Sir
Desmond
MacCarthy

Cecilia,
m. Adm.
Sir Willia
Fisher

Michael,
d. 1973

Rachel,
m. Lord
David
Cecil

Dermod

APPENDIX A

James Pattle was the fourth son of Thomas Pattle (1748/9–1818) and Sarah Hasleby Pattle (1754–1813), who were married in Bengal on June 10, 1770 (*Bengal: Past and Present*, 1909, IV, 510). Mr. Thomas Pattle was an important member of the Bengal Civil Service under Warren Hastings and Richard Barwell, and after twenty years in Calcutta (first appointed July 16, 1765, according to the *Bengal Kalendar and Register . . . 1800*, p. 3), he returned to London, 1779, for a decade as a Director of the Hon. E. I. Co., elected 1787 and 1792 to represent the Indian interests. See C. H. Philips, *The East India Company 1784–1834* (Manchester: Manchester University Press, 1940), p. 337. In 1795, disqualified for re-election, he went back to Calcutta, received a rousing welcome from his old friends at the annual St. Andrew's Day banquet, and proceeded to his post as Senior Judge of the Court of Appeal in Murshidabad, some distance up the Ganges (W. S. Seton-Kerr, ed., *Selections from Calcutta Gazettes*, II, 435–6; III, 285 and 311; and *Bengal Kalendar . . . 1800*, p. 3). There he still was in 1801–2, when he entertained Wellesley at his home; but a few years later he was transferred to the judgeship of the District of Cawnpore. The Pattles, apparently a London family, though not so conspicuous as some, were thought worthy to be mentioned among Anglo-Indian families in the same breath with Plowdens and Prinseps; see Sir John William Kaye, *Life of Lord Metcalfe* (London, 1858), I, 5. Their name appears occasionally in eighteenth-century East-Indian records, beginning with Edward Pattle, B.C.S., 1692–1715. They were typical minor nabobs, rolling up the customary fortune, which Mr. James Pattle is said to have left to his daughters.

APPENDIX B

'The Chevalier de l'Etang: A Romantic Figure of Old France', *The Connoisseur* (July 1925), pp. 177–8, includes a coloured reproduction of a miniature of the Pattle girls' grandfather, Ambroise Pierre Antoine de l'Etang (1757–1840), knight of the Order of St. Louis. Antoine de l'Etang, like his father before him, had grown up in the service of the French royal family, as an officer of the Garde du Corps, Superintendent of the Stud of Louis XVI, and a page of honour of Marie Antoinette. See V. C. P. Hodson, *List of the Officers of the Bengal Army, 1758–1834* (London: Constable & Co., 1928), II, 44. Some time between Oct. 1787, when he was refused permission to marry, and May 1791, when he appears as 'cousin par alliance' of the Blin de Grincourt family in Pondicherry, Antoine de l'Etang, now an officer in the Spahis, married Thérèse Blin de Grincourt, a maid of honour to Marie Antoinette and renowned for her beauty. See *Catalogue des Manuscrits des Anciennes Archives de l'Inde Française, Pondichéry, 1609–1789*, ed. Edmond Gaudart (Paris: Editions Leroux, 1926), I, 379; and *Arrêts du Conseil Supérieur de Pondichéry*, ed. Gnanou Diagou (Paris: Ernest Leroux, 1937), V (1790–4), 180.

The numerous Blin family were important in Pondicherry, and l'Etang appears frequently in its surviving records in positions of responsibility and honour between May 1791 and April 1792. But the same records suggest by their silence that the couple had left Pondicherry and were not present at its siege and capitulation to the British in 1793. Whether l'Etang was elsewhere in India on military duty, or had returned to the service of the Queen in Paris is not recorded, but family tradition says that he was present with Marie Antoinette in her imprisonment and at her execution in 1793, and avoiding a *lettre de cachet*, escaped with his wife to India, where he remained the rest of his life. Family Records; see also Mrs. Colin Mackenzie, *Storms and Sunshine of a Soldier's Life* (Edinburgh, 1884), I, 25.

Antoine de l'Etang next turns up in Calcutta in 1796, and in 1800 was Master of the Riding School (*Bengal Kalendar . . . 1800*, 'List of

Europeans, not in the service of his Majesty, or the Company');
from Feb. 1802 to Dec. 1805, he was Veterinary Surgeon to the
Governor-General's Body Guard (Family Records), and in 1807
seems to have been responsible in some capacity for the Hon. Co.'s
horses and vehicles (*Selections from Calcutta Gazettes*, IV, 423),
probably already enjoying his appointment as a junior officer in
the Stud Department. As a veterinary surgeon and expert horseman,
he doubtless made an excellent living in sporting and military
Calcutta. He left the Hon. Co.'s Stud Dept. for a brief time in 1814
entering a similar position in the service of the Nawab of Oudh,
but soon returned to the former post. See *The Private Journal of the
Marquess of Hastings* (London, 1858), I, 212–22. Eventually he
received appointment as '1st Asst. in the Hon. Company's Stud
Dept.' in 1827 at Buxhar (Hodson, II, 44), from Lord William
Bentinck, the governor-general whose favourite he was said to have
been. From there he moved up to head the Stud Dept. at Ghazipur.
Mackenzie, his grandson-in-law, met the old gentleman for the first
time in July 1840 at Ghazipur, a few months before l'Etang's death,
and described him as 'an excellent specimen of a French gentleman
of the old school' (Mackenzie, I, 104).

The l'Etangs had two sons, who did not survive their parents;
one of them, Eugene, born at Palta near Barrackpur in 1803, entered
his Majesty's forces, was stationed with his father at Buxhar, and
died in 1829 (Hodson, II, 44). The three l'Etang daughters were
educated near Paris in the aristocratic school conducted by Madame
Campan (Mackenzie, I, 25), and, rejoining their parents in India,
were promptly married off to members of the Bengal Civil Service:
Adeline, probably the eldest, to James Pattle; another to an Impey,
probably Edward Impey, youngest son of Sir Elijah; and the third
to Samuel Beadle. Their mother, Mme. Thérèse de l'Etang, according to the custom of European officers' wives as soon as their offspring
had been well established, retired from India to live in Versailles.

APPENDIX C

J. H. Siddons, in *Memoirs of a Journalist*, p. 100, wrote: 'There were some curious specimens of the seniors of the service then in Calcutta. Two of the judges enjoyed severally the soubriquets of "Stupid Bob" and "Booby M."; and a third, whose private propensities were more frequently objects of remark, than his public acts were themes of admiration, was popularly known by the not very intelligible appellation of "Jemmy Blazes", But H. G. Keene, arriving in Calcutta only a few months after Mr. Pattle's death, says that it was Col. William Pattle who was 'familiarly known as "Jemmy Blazes"'; see his *Here and There, Memories Indian and Other* (London: Brown, Langham & Co., 1906), p. 42. Mr. Keene continues: Col. Pattle 'had been somewhat notorious a few years before' 1846 'on account of his prowess as a raconteur, and many were the anecdotes about him which were still current in those days. He had risen in the 9th Bengal Light Cavalry, and commanded the corps at the battle of Miani, where Sir Charles Napier broke the resistance of the Amirs of Sindh in 1843. *Miyan* is the Persian for "scabbard", and it was related that the Colonel accounted for the name of the field in some such terms as these: "In the thick of the mêlée Sir Charles rode up to me, crying, 'By G—, Colonel, this is butchery; give me your sword, sir!' I had, of course to obey; but my blood was up. Calling on my men to follow, I returned to the charge—and you may believe me or not— killed eleven of the enemy with my empty scabbard. Hence the name." '

The full story of what happened to Col. Pattle at Miani, when twenty-five hundred British troops beat thirty to forty thousand Baluchis, has recently been unearthed. Sir Charles sent the colonel, his second in command, not one but two orders to charge with all the force of the cavalry at the crisis of the battle. But the elderly colonel, 'who was rather deaf' and 'could not hear what was said in the din of battle', and besides, though 'brave', was a 'somewhat unintelligent man', hesitated in a fog of military punctilio, until the rumour got started that he had refused to comply. Jacob's Horse and one squadron of Pattle's took the lead, and then Pattle leading the rest 'gallantly attacked' and the battle was won. See H. T. Lambricke, *Sir Charles Napier and Sind* (Oxford: Clarendon Press, 1952), pp. 145-146. As for Napier's sword, the general wrote his brother, 'Our dear father's sword which I wore' at Miani 'is unstained, even with blood, for I did not kill any one with my own hand.' On the strength of his Sind campaign, Col. Pattle won a C.B., the colonelcy of the 4th Light Cavalry, and eventually a position as aide de camp to the Queen, with the rank of General (Family Records).

BIBLIOGRAPHY

Annan, Noel Gilroy, Lord. *Leslie Stephen: His Thought and Character in Relation to His Time*. Cambridge: Harvard University Press, 1952.

Appointments in Bengal and Their Holders from About the Year 1850 Down to 1902. Calcutta: Bengal Secretariat Press, 1903.

Askwith, Betty. *Two Victorian Families*, London: Chatto & Windus, 1971.

Balfour, Lady Betty, ed. *Personal and Literary Letters of Robert First Earl of Lytton*. London: Longmans, Green & Co., 1906. 2 vols.

Bell, Clive. *Old Friends: Personal Recollections*. London: Chatto & Windus, 1956.

Bell, Quentin. *Bloomsbury*. London: Weidenfeld & Nicolson, 1968.

—, *Virginia Woolf: A Biography*. Vol. I, *Virginia Stephen, 1882–1912*, London: The Hogarth Press, 1972.

Bengal and Agra Annual Guide and Gazetter, 1841–1842. 4 vols. Vol. I, 3rd ed.

Bengal Kalendar and Register for the Year 1800. Calcutta: Mirror Press, 1800.

Bengal Obituary . . . , The. Calcutta: Holmes & Co., London: W. Thacker & Co., 1851.

Bengal: Past and Present. Journal of the Calcutta Historical Society. Vol. I, 1907–.

Benson, E. F. *As We Were; A Victorian Peepshow*. London: Longmans, Green & Co., 1931.

Blunt, Wilfrid. *'England's Michelangelo': A Biography of George Frederic Watts, O.M., R.A.* London: Hamish Hamilton, 1975.

Buckland, C. E. *Bengal Under the Lieutenant-Governors*. Calcutta: S. K. Lahiri & Co., 1901. 2 vols.

Carey, W. H. *The Good Old Days of Honourable John Company*. Calcutta: R. Cambrey & Co., 1906. 2 vols.

Carrington: Letters and Extracts From Her Diaries. Ed. David Garnett. London: Jonathan Cape, 1970.

Chapman, Ronald. *The Laurel and the Thorn, A Study of G. F. Watts*. London: Faber & Faber, 1945.

Clark, Francis, comp. *The East-India Register and Army List, 1845–1860*. London: W. H. Allen, 1949. Vols for 1849 and 1851.

Cornish, Vaughan. *A Family of Devon, Their Homes, Travels, and Occupations.* St. Leonard's-on-Sea, Sussex: King Bros. & Potts Ltd., 1942.

—. *Kestell, Clapp, and Cornish; Records of Home Life and Travel.* London: Sifton Praed, 1947.

Cotton, H. E. A. *Calcutta Old and New.* Calcutta: W. Newman & Co., 1907.

Crawford, Lt.-Col. D. F. *Roll of the Indian Medical Service 1615–1930.* London: W. Thacker & Co., 1930.

Curzon of Kedleston, George Nathaniel, Lord. *British Government in India.* London: Cassell & Co., 1925. 2 vols.

Duberman, Martin. *James Russell Lowell.* Boston: Houghton Mifflin, 1966.

Dupree, A. Hunter. *Asa Gray, 1810–1888.* Cambridge: Belknap Press Harvard University Press, 1959.

Eden, Hon. Emily. *Letters From India.* London: Richard Bentley & Son, 1872. 2 vols.

—. *Miss Eden's Letters.* Ed. Violet Dickinson. London: Macmillan, 1919.

Fawcett, Dame Millicent Garrett. *What I Remember.* London: T. Fisher Unwin, Ltd., 1924.

Fifoot, C. H. S. *Frederic William Maitland: A Life.* Cambridge: Harvard University Press, 1971.

Forster, E. M. *Two Cheers For Democracy.* New York: Harcourt, Brace & Co., 1951.

Foster, Sir William. *John Company.* London: John Lane and the Bodley Head, Ltd., 1926.

Fraser, Sir William. *The Chiefs of Grant.* London and Edinburgh, 1883. 3 vols.

Fuller, Hester Thackeray and V. Hammersley, comps. *Thackeray's Daughter; Some Recollections.* Dublin: Euphorion Books, 1951.

Garnett, David. *The Flowers of the Forest.* New York: Harcourt, Brace & Co., 1955.

Gathorne-Hardy, Robert. *Recollections of Logan Pearsall Smith: the Story of a Friendship.* New York: Macmillan, 1950.

Gernsheim, Helmut. *Julia Margaret Cameron: Her Life and Photographic Art.* Introd. by Clive Bell. London: The Fountain Press, 1948.

Grant, Anne. *Memoir and Correspondence of Mrs. Grant of Laggan.* Ed. J. P. Grant. London: Longmans, 1844. 3 vols.

Gray, Asa. *Letters of Asa Gray.* Ed. Jane Loring Gray. Boston: Houghton Mifflin, 1893. 2 vols.

Greenslet, Ferris. *The Lowells and Their Seven Worlds.* Boston: Houghton Mifflin, 1946.

Hare, A. C. *The Story of Two Noble Lives*. London: George Allen, 1893. 3 vols.

Harrod, R. F. *The Life of John Maynard Keynes*. New York: Harcourt, Brace & Co., 1951.

Hill, Brian. *Julia Margaret Cameron: A Victorian Family Portrait*. London: Peter Owen, 1973.

Holroyd, Michael. *Lytton Strachey: A Critical Biography*. London: Heinemann, 1967-8. 2 vols.

Huie, Jennie. 'Anne Thackeray (afterwards Lady Ritchie),' unpublished dissertation, London University, 1960.

Hunter, W. H. *The Thackerays in India*. London: Henry Frowde, 1897.

Huxley, Leonard. *Life and Letters of Sir Joseph Dalton Hooker*. London: John Murray, 1918. 2 vols.

James, Henry. *The Selected Letters of Henry James*. Ed. with an introd. by Leon Edel. New York: Farrar, Straus & Cudahy, 1955.

Johnstone, J. K. *The Bloomsbury Group*. London: Secker & Warburg, 1954.

Kaye, John William. *A History of the Sepoy War in India, 1857-1858*. 9th ed. London: W. H. Allen & Co., 1880. 3 vols.

Keene, H. G. *Here and There, Memories Indian and Other*. London: Brown, Langham & Co., 1906.

Laurie, W. F. B. *Sketches of Some Distinguished Anglo-Indians*. London: W. H. Allen & Co., 1887. Revised ed.

Lee-Warner, Sir William. *Life of the Marquis of Dalhousie*. London: Macmillan, 1904. 2 vols.

Leigh-Smith, Philip. *Record of an Ascent: A Memoir of Sir Richmond Thackeray Ritchie*. London: Dillon's University Bookshop, Ltd., 1961.

Leveson-Gower, Hon. E. Frederick. *Bygone Years* . . . . London: John Murray, 1905.

Lowell, James Russell. *Letters of James Russell Lowell*. Ed. C. E. Norton. London: Osgood, McIlvaine & Co., 1894. 2 vols.

Lubbock, Percy. *Shades of Eton*. London: Jonathan Cape, 1929.

MacCarthy, Sir Desmond. *Leslie Stephen*. Cambridge, 1937.

——. *Memories*. New York: Oxford University Press, 1953.

——. *Portraits*. New York: Macmillan, 1932.

MacCarthy, Mary Josefa Warre-Cornish, Lady. *The Festival*. London: Longmans, Green, 1937.

——. *Fighting Fitzgerald . . . and Other Papers*. London: Martin Secker, 1930.

——. *Handicaps. Six Studies*. London: Longmans, Green, 1936.

——. *A Nineteenth-Century Childhood*. London: Martin Secker, New Adelphi Library, 1929. Revised ed.

—. *A Pier and A Band,* with introd. by David Garnett. London: Martin Secker, New Adelphi Library, 1931. 2nd ed.

Mackenzie, Helen (Mrs. Colin). *Storms and Sunshine of a Soldier's Life: Lt.-Gen. C. Mackenzie.* Edinburgh, 1884. 2 vols.

Maitland, F. W. *Life and Letters of Leslie Stephen.* London: Duckworth & Co., 1906.

Malleson, George Bruce. *History of the Indian Mutiny, 1857–58.* London: W. H. Allen & Co., 1878 and 1880. 3 vols.

Merivale, Charles. *Autobiography of Dean Merivale: with Selections from His Correspondence.* Ed. Judith Anne Merivale. London: Edward Arnold, 1899.

Morrell, Lady Ottoline. *Memoirs of Lady Ottoline Morrell. A Study in Friendship 1873–1915.* Ed. Robert Gathorne-Hardy. New York: A. A. Knopf, 1964.

Morris, Henry. *The Life of Charles Grant.* London: John Murray, 1904.

Philips, C. H. *The East India Company 1784–1834.* Manchester: Manchester University Press, 1940.

Pippett, Aileen. *The Moth and the Star: A Biography of Virginia Woolf.* Boston: Little, Brown & Co., 1955.

Plowden, Walter F. C. Chicheley. *Records of the Chicheley Plowdens, A.D. 1590–1913.* London: Heath, Cranton & Ouseley, Ltd., 1914.

Preus, O. J. H. 'Anne Thackeray Ritchie and the Victorian Literary Aristocracy', dissertation available on microfilm, University of Minnesota, 1959.

Proceedings of the Massachusetts Historical Society, 2nd series, Vol. 18, 1903–4.

Rawlinson, H. G., ed. *Personal Reminiscences of Augusta Becher, 1830–1888.* London: Constable & Co., Ltd., 1930.

Ray, Gordon. *Thackeray: The Uses of Adversity* and *The Age of Wisdom.* London: Oxford University Press, 1955, 1958. 2 vols.

Ritchie, Anne Isabella Thackeray, Lady. *Alfred, Lord Tennyson and His Friends . . . 25 Portraits* (by) *Mrs. Julia Margaret Cameron and H. H. H. Cameron.* London: T. F. Unwin, 1893.

—. *A Book of Sybils.* London: Smith, Elder & Co., 1883.

—. *Chapters From Some Memoirs.* London: Macmillan, 1894.

—. *From Friend to Friend.* Ed. Emily Ritchie. London: John Murray, 1919.

—. *From the Porch.* London: Smith, Elder & Co., 1913.

—. *Letters of Anne Thackeray Ritchie.* Ed. Hester Ritchie. London: John Murray, 1924.

—. *Mrs. Dymond.* London: Smith, Elder & Co., 1885.

—. *Old Kensington.* London: Smith, Elder & Co., 1873. 2nd ed.

—. *Tennyson, Ruskin, and Browning.* London: Macmillan, 1892.

Ritchie, Anne Isabella Thackeray, Lady. 'Thackeray and His Biographers', in *Illustrated London News*, Vol. 98 (June 20, 1891), p. 811.

—. *Toilers and Spinsters and Other Essays*. London: Smith, Elder & Co., 1874.

Ritchie, Gerald. *The Ritchies in India*. London: John Murray, 1920.

Roberts, Emma. *Scenes and Characters of Hindostan, with Sketches of Anglo-Indian Society*. London, 1835. 3 vols.

Rothenstein, William. *Men and Memories . . . 1872–1900*. New York: Coward-McCann, Inc., 1935.

Sandeman, Hugh David, ed. *Selections from Calcutta Gazettes*. Calcutta: Supt. of Govt. Printing, 1869. Vol. V (1816–23).

Sanders, Charles Richard. *The Strachey Family, 1588–1932*. Durham: Duke University Press, 1953.

Seton-Kerr, Walter Scott. *Grant of Rothiemurchus*. London: John Murray, 1899.

—. *Selections from Calcutta Gazettes, 1789–97*. London: Longmans, Green, Reeder & Dyer, 1865. 2 vols.

Siddons, J. H. (pseud. Stocqueler). *Memoirs of a Journalist*. Bombay, 1873.

Simpson, Minnie Nassau Senior (Mrs. M. C.). *Many Memories of Many People*. London: Edward Arnold, 1898. 4th ed.

Smith, Mrs. Eliza Grant. *Memoirs of a Highland Lady*. Ed. Lady Strachey. London: John Murray, 1898.

Smith, Elizabeth Blakeway. *George Smith, A Memoir*. London: Smith, Elder & Co., 1902.

Smith, Logan Pearsall. *Unforgotten Years*. London: Constable & Co., Ltd., 1938.

Smyth, Dame Ethel Mary. *Impressions That Remained*. New York: Knopf, 1946.

Spender, Stephen. *World Within World*. New York: Harcourt, Brace & Co., 1951.

Stephen, Sir Leslie. *The Life of Sir James Fitzjames Stephen*. London: Smith, Elder & Co., 1895.

—. *Social Rights and Duties: Addresses to Ethical Societies*. New York: Macmillan & Co., 1896. 2 vols.

Strachey, Jane Maria Grant, Lady. *Lay Texts for the Young in English and French*. 1887.

—. *Nursery Lyrics*. London: Chatto & Windus, 1922. 2nd ed.

—. *Poets on Poets*. London: Kegan, Paul, Trench, Trubner & Co., 1894.

Strachey, Sir John. *India: Its Administration and Progress*. London: Macmillan & Co., 1903. 3rd ed. revised and enlarged.

—, and Lt-.Gen. Richard Strachey. *The Finances and Public Works of India*. London: Kegan, Paul, Trench & Co., 1882.

Strachey, Ray. *Millicent Garrett Fawcett*. London: John Murray, 1931.

Tayler, William. *Thirty-Eight Years in India*. London: W. H. Allen & Co., 1882. 2 vols.

Taylor, Una. *Guests and Memories*. London: Humphrey Milford, Oxford University Press, 1924.

Tennyson, Hallam, Lord. *Alfred Lord Tennyson, A Memoir*. London: Macmillan & Co., 1906.

—, ed. *Tennyson and His Friends*. London: Macmillan, 1911.

Thackeray, William Makepeace. *The Letters and Private Papers of William Makepeace Thackeray*. Ed. Gordon N. Ray. Cambridge: Harvard University Press, 1945–6. 4 vols.

—. *The Oxford Thackeray: Miscellaneous Contributions to Punch, 1843–1854*. Ed. George Saintsbury. London: Oxford University Press, n.d.

Trevelyan, G. O. *The Life and Letters of Lord Macaulay*. New York: Harper & Bros., 1876. 2 vols.

Troubridge, Laura Gurney, Lady. *Memories and Reflections*. London: William Heinemann, 1925.

Victorian Photographs of Famous Men and Fair Women. With introductions by Virginia Woolf and Roger Fry. New York: Harcourt, Brace & Co., 1926.

Ward, Wilfrid. *Aubrey de Vere: A Memoir*. London: Longmans, Green & Co., 1904.

—. *Men and Matters*. London: Longmans, Green & Co., 1914.

Warre-Cornish, Blanche Ritchie. *Some Family Letters of W. M. Thackeray, together with Recollections by His Kinswoman*. Boston: Houghton Mifflin Co., 1911.

Warre-Cornish, Francis Thackeray. *Letters and Sketches of Francis T. Warre-Cornish, Late Capt. 17th Bengal Lancers . . . 1884–1901*. Ed. Francis T. Warre-Cornish. Eton: Spottiswoode & Co., 1902.

Watts, M. S. *George Frederic Watts; the Annals of an Artist's Life*. London: Macmillan, 1912. 2 vols.

Weld, Agnes Grace. *Glimpses of Tennyson and of Some of His Relations and Friends*. London: Williams and Norgate, 1903.

Woolf, Leonard. *Beginning Again: An Autobiography of the Years 1911 to 1918*. New York: Harcourt, Brace & World, Inc., 1963.

—, *Sowing, an Autobiography of the Years 1880 to 1904*. London: The Hogarth Press, 1960.

—. *The Wise Virgins: A Story of Words, Opinions, and a Few Emotions*. London: Edward Arnold, 1914.

Woolf, Virginia. 'The Enchanted Organ', in *The Moment and Other Essays*. London: Hogarth Press, 1947.

—. 'Lady Strachey', in *The Nation and the Athenaeum*, Vol. 44 (Dec. 22, 1928), pp. 441–2.

Woolf, Virginia. 'Leslie Stephen', in *The Captain's Deathbed*. New York: Harcourt, Brace & Co., 1950.
—. *Night and Day*. London: The Hogarth Press, 1919.
—. *To the Lighthouse*. New York: Harcourt, Brace & Co., 1927.
—. *A Writer's Diary*. Ed. Leonard Woolf. New York: Harcourt, Brace & Co., 1953.
Zuckerman, Joanne P. 'Anne Thackeray Ritchie as the Model for Mrs. Hilbery in Virginia Woolf's *Night and Day*', *Virginia Woolf Quarterly*, Spring 1973, Vol. I, No. 3, pp. 32–46.

INDEX